Don't Pay for Your

MBA

Don't Pay for Your

The Faster, Cheaper, Better Way
to Get the Business Education You Need

LAURIE PICKARD

AMACOM

AMERICAN MANAGEMENT ASSOCIATION
New York • Atlanta • Brussels • Chicago • Mexico City
San Francisco • Shanghai • Tokyo • Toronto • Washington, DC

Bulk discounts available. For details visit:
www.amacombooks.org/go/specialsales
Or contact special sales:
Phone: 800-250-5308
E-mail: specialsls@amanet.org
View all the AMACOM titles at: www.amacombooks.org
American Management Association: www.amanet.org

This publication is designed to provide accurate and authoritative information in regard to the subject matter covered. It is sold with the understanding that the publisher is not engaged in rendering legal, accounting, or other professional service. If legal advice or other expert assistance is required, the services of a competent professional person should be sought.

Library of Congress Cataloging-in-Publication Data

Names: Pickard, Laurie, author.
Title: Don't pay for your MBA : the faster, cheaper, better way to get the
   business education you need / Laurie Pickard.
Description: New York, NY : AMACOM, [2017] | Includes index.
Identifiers: LCCN 2017018326 (print) | LCCN 2017038072 (ebook) | ISBN
   9780814438497 (eBook) | ISBN 9780814438480 (pbk.)
Subjects: LCSH: Master of business administration degree. | Management--Study
   and teaching (Higher)
Classification: LCC HF1111 (ebook) | LCC HF1111 .P53 2017 (print) | DDC
   658.0071/1--dc23
LC record available at https://lccn.loc.gov/2017018326

About AMA
American Management Association (www.amanet.org) is a world leader in talent development, advancing the skills of individuals to drive business success. Our mission is to support the goals of individuals and organizations through a complete range of products and services, including classroom and virtual seminars, webcasts, webinars, podcasts, conferences, corporate and government solutions, business books, and research. AMA's approach to improving performance combines experiential learning—learning through doing—with opportunities for ongoing professional growth at every step of one's career journey.

10 9 8 7 6 5 4 3 2 1

CONTENTS

INTRODUCTION

MOOC Your MBA

"Our ability to learn what we need for tomorrow is more important than what we know today."

—GEORGE SIEMENS

This book traces its birth to a balmy evening in 2013. I had just finished a three-year assignment as a Peace Corps volunteer in the rural countryside of Nicaragua. Now living in Nicaragua's capital, Managua, I was barely scraping by as a part-time consultant for the local branch of the World Bank. Having worked for nearly four years for low and sometimes no wages, I was eager to land a proper job in international development and make some decent money. Searching online through endless job postings, I grew more and more depressed. Nothing seemed to match my resume: a BA in politics, an MA in geography, years of volunteer service, and a brief stint as a project manager.

Every international development job, it seemed, called for a degree in business, finance, or economics. I began to wonder if, rather than looking for a job, I should cut to the chase and start researching MBA programs. Newly married, I was excited to join my husband as he pursued his career in foreign aid. That meant a lot of globe-trotting, as new assignments took us to far-flung corners of the world. I had concluded that my own career depended on getting a first-class business education, but how on earth would I pay for it? I couldn't saddle my new marriage and my early career with huge student debt.

Quite unexpectedly, the answer to my dilemma showed up on my doorstep. My husband and I were enjoying a chat with our friend Julio on the patio of our house, tossing around ideas about our future prospects. Julio could barely contain his excitement about his recent experience with MOOCs. "*Mooks?*" I asked. He laughed, "Spelled M-O-O-C. It stands for massive open online course. I'm taking one to brush up on finance. You wouldn't believe it. The professor teaches at NYU, and he's famous for his work on corporate valuation. It's truly world-class. And it doesn't cost a dime! I've taken a look at other courses from Wharton, MIT, and Stanford. I could practically refresh my MBA with the courses that are out there."

I felt a big electric charge when I heard that. Imagine studying with the world's top professors for the price of an Internet connection! I could picture myself earning the equivalent of an Ivy League MBA while sitting under a palm tree or on a beach blanket in Southern France.

The next morning I popped open my laptop and typed in "Free online business courses." Wow! The options amazed me. I could study management, marketing, finance, accounting, human resources, operations, innovation, and entrepreneurship with professors at the world's best business schools. Could I actually stitch together enough of these courses to fashion my own tailor-made degree in business? I could. And I did! I chronicled the entire journey in a blog called "No-Pay MBA."

Fast-forward three years. I now live with my husband in the small East African nation of Rwanda, applying my self-made, just-in-time business education as a private-sector development adviser in the offices of the United States Agency for International Development. I make a good income and spend a lot of time moonlighting as an adviser to all of the learners worldwide who read and subscribe to my No-Pay MBA blog. I have written about the subject of self-directed business education for the *Financial Times*, been quoted in the *Wall Street Journal* and *Bloomberg Business*, and received write-ups in both *Fortune* and *Entrepreneur*. My nontraditional business education has opened many doors.

You probably bought this book because you are already thinking about pursuing your own nontraditional business education. If so, you could probably use a guide through the nooks and crannies of this phenomenal new way to obtain your own self-tailored No-Pay MBA. I will be delighted to serve as that guide.

Welcome to the Future of Education and Work

In the digital age, business education has gone viral. No longer locked securely behind the ivied halls of elite universities, the knowledge, skills, and frameworks that make up a first-class business education have become virtually free and available to anyone with a laptop and an Internet connection. Welcome to the wonderful world of online business education: massive open online courses (MOOCs) offered by elite schools, short training courses produced by industry professionals, and talks by world experts, all available with a tap on the keypad or a click of a mouse.

And the revolution has arrived just in time. In today's rapidly evolving job market, current and prospective workers need to learn and apply new skills throughout their working lives. In 2015 the Bureau of Labor Statistics reported that over the course of one's career the average worker born between 1957 and 1964 had held 11.7 jobs, spending less than five years in each position.[1] Those following in their footsteps will need to retool themselves continually throughout their careers. If you don't want to risk ending up in the breakdown lane of the information highway, you'd better figure out how to keep your skills fresh and relevant. Let's face it: The degree you earn in your twenties no longer guarantees gainful employment throughout a forty-plus-year career.

If you pursued an MBA the regular way, you'd end up taking a lot of required courses that you may or may not be able to use right away. Years later, would you remember what you studied in Supply Chain Management 101? Worse yet, what if you never ended up needing that information at all? Still, business students in traditional programs must invest valuable time and money to complete course requirements that may or may not fit their particular situations. Instead, why not tailor your business education to fit your unique and specific needs? Professor George Siedel, who teaches a popular MOOC on negotiation, once described traditional business school as a "just in case" education, where students learn most topics "just in case" they might come in handy later. But "just in case" doesn't square with the world of work that we now inhabit. Increasingly, people need skills that can be acquired and refreshed "just in time." New educational tools like MOOCs can not only help you acquire specific skills just when you need them, they can refresh a skill that has faded over time. Revisiting a course like Professor Siedel's before your next salary negotiation could mean the difference between a lackluster package and a competitive one.

Employers, too, have begun to value more than conventional degrees, university brand names, and even academic grades, none of which guarantee superior performance on the job. Just take a look at Google, one of the hottest employers in the world. Laszlo Bock, senior vice president of People Operations at Google, discusses the company's hiring practices in his 2015 book *Work Rules!* As Bock explains, at Google, "The pedigree of your college education matters far less than what you have accomplished. For some roles, it's not important whether you went at all. What matters is what you bring to the company and how you've distinguished yourself."[2]

Together, these irresistible forces (the easy availability of information, the fast-changing workplace, and the shifting importance of traditional degrees) have conspired to erode the value of a traditional MBA degree. Add to that the fact that an MBA has never been a required degree. There is no law requiring a degree of any kind to practice business; it's not like the degrees you need to practice medicine or law. As executive coach and professor at Stanford's Graduate School of Business, Ed Batista explained in *The Harvard Business Review*, "[The MBA is] an optional degree and is nothing like a JD, an MD, or the other credentials that professions such as law and medicine make mandatory. There are many senior people in general management roles, in consulting, and even in financial services who don't have an MBA—so don't assume that the credential will necessarily serve a meaningful purpose in your chosen field."[3]

Yet the MBA remains popular because it promises what a liberal arts degree once supposedly guaranteed: a soft landing in the hard world of finding a job and managing a career. While you may find that prospect alluring, it guarantees nothing. Consider the fact that while many MBA grads do start out with more sizable salaries than those without that credential, not all do. Graduates from mid- or lower-tier programs may not see their job prospects improved at all. At San Diego State University, over 50 percent of the MBA class of 2015 still had not found jobs three months after graduation.[4] And not all MBAs who do find jobs score six-figure salaries. Those who work for startups, nonprofits, or the government, or who switch fields and end up in lower-level positions, make significantly less.

Then consider that the average total cost of a two-year, traditional MBA program in the United States now tops $150,000. If you end up at a highly ranked MBA program, such as the Wharton School of Business, the sum total of tuition, living expenses, and opportunity costs (in the form of lost salary) could run up to a whopping $220,000![5] Even part-time and online programs can cost in the neighborhood of $75,000. None of these options work for people who do not wish to find themselves buried under a mountain of student debt, especially when other options cost so much less. As you follow the program presented in this book, you will find out how you can pursue those options in a way that costs you less and earns you more.

Rebundle Your Business Education

When universities began offering their courses online at little or no cost, they began a revolution that Anant Agarwal, the CEO of the MOOC platform edX, has called "the unbundling of education."[6] Just as high-speed Internet comes bundled with cable television, university education comes bundled with career services and the campus quad. The big benefit of unbundling is that it allows consumers to pay for exactly and only what they need, resulting in substantial savings. In the pages ahead you will learn how to assemble a customized business education that will give you the biggest bang for your hard-earned bucks.

The road to success with self-directed education parallels the traditional path. It starts with the admissions process, where you ask yourself the same sort of questions you'd find on a college admissions form. For example, "What am I hoping to achieve through my education?" Chapter 1 walks you through your personal admissions process.

Chapter 2 familiarizes you with MOOCs, the learning technology that will make your nontraditional, self-directed MBA possible. Once admitted to your virtual MBA program, you pick and choose your coursework from the ever-expanding MOOC catalog. Whatever specific curriculum you design for yourself, you will want to master the common language of business. Chapter 3 teaches you how to build that foundation with core business concepts.

Concepts are fine; but skills are even better. In a perfect world, conventional business school students learn a wide-ranging set of skills that prepare them to understand complex situations, make data-driven decisions, and lead teams of people. In your nontraditional program you can do the same. That's the subject of Chapter 4.

Most MBA programs help students, especially those who have recently enrolled, figure out what kind of career will suit them best. Guidance counselors, advisers, coaches, and mentors strive to match the hand with the glove. One size does not fit all—a problem that a No-Pay MBA can solve better than a traditional program. Chapter 5 shows you how to tailor your education toward the career with the best possible fit.

Real estate people talk about the importance of location, location, location. In business it's all about network, network, network. Graduates from traditional MBA programs often believe that the network they built as students outweighed what they learned in the classroom. Chapter 6 will teach you techniques for building a strong business network of your own.

In the second year of many traditional MBA programs, students begin to concentrate on one particular subject area, be it marketing, management, finance, entrepreneurship, supply chain dynamics, or any of the other major disciplines. In Chapter 7, you will learn how to select your own focus, developing deep functional expertise through advanced coursework and real-world experience.

Of course, the letters MBA still impress people. But that doesn't mean you must take a back seat to three capital letters. Increasingly, employers value self-motivated, hardworking, eager learners. You just need to package your No-Pay MBA in a way that will make a boss, a potential employer, or a would-be investor sit up and take notice. In Chapter 8, you'll plan your strategy for communicating your nontraditional education in just the right way. You have prepared yourself for that promotion, that new job, that startup venture. In Chapter 8, you will learn how to communicate your self-directed education in a way that will impress future employers, even without a piece of paper bearing a $100,000 price tag.

Finally, Chapter 9 will encourage you to remain on the lifelong learning path, even after you have finished the business education you need to reach your initial goals. It discusses the importance of continually sharpening your skills both online and on the job, adopting an international perspective through both actual and virtual travel, developing a Lifelong Learning Plan, and interacting with and encouraging future generations of independent learners.

Enroll Today

This book distills everything I have learned taking apart the old-school approach to business education and putting it back together in a way that can empower you to get ahead in whatever business career you've chosen or will choose in the future. You can think of me as your personal MBA adviser, the sort of mentor and champion usually included in a traditional brick-and-mortar MBA program. Throughout this book, you will find Adviser's Challenges that will help you take concrete steps toward your goal of acquiring a top-notch, self-directed MBA.

As a result of my work with business students around the world, many of whom you will meet in the pages ahead, I have come to believe that we are poised on the brink of an Educational Revolution that will transform the world and work opportunities every bit as much as the Industrial and Information Revolutions did. It has already begun. It's global. And it's only accelerating. Ignore it at your peril, or embrace it to change your life.

I have drawn the stories in this book from the scores of people who have inspired me with their self-designed approaches to independent learning. They include Kristof, a banker who studies business from Belgium; Hillary, an entrepreneur and single mom who takes online courses in California; and Ellen, an arts administrator in New York. Although they have never met in person, Kristof and Hillary have become close friends and collaborators during their studies. At the time of this writing, they are taking a course on small business financing, using Hillary's business as a case study. Ellen became passionate about negotiation after taking an online course on the subject. Inspired by what she had learned, she has volunteered her services to a community initiative that teaches women how to become better negotiators. Note that I have not used the last names of the people whose stories I have included in this book. In many cases I have also changed a first name or modified the details of a story to protect that person's privacy. (Same goes for some of the names of the companies where these learners work.) I love these true stories of hardworking self-starters who are using self-directed learning methods to take control of their own business success. I can't wait to add *your* success story to my collection. You will find additional resources to accompany this book, as well as multiple ways to get in touch with me, at my website, NoPayMBA.com.

1

Prep for Success

Administering Your Own Admissions Process

KRISTOF felt stuck. After graduating with his master's degree in economics, he started his career in banking with a sense of possibility and adventure. He loved the idea of applying the concepts he had spent the past five years studying. His first job as an international management trainee at Fortis Bank gave him that chance. Rotating through several departments, he soaked up new skills and knowledge like a sponge, but when he landed in the trading room, he felt he had finally found his home in the banking world. In the aftermath of the 2008 financial crisis, Fortis fell into the hands of a much larger rival, BNP Paribas. Despite numerous layoffs, Kristof kept his job. However, the culture at work changed as people, worried about losing their jobs, worked feverishly to achieve higher and higher returns in a bleak market. Long hours and frequent weekend stints added to the strain and left little room for family time. While Kristof still loved economics and finance, many of the exciting possibilities he had envisioned were beginning to fade. All work and no play made for a very dull day. Something had to give.

Could an MBA reignite his passion and open up exciting new possibilities? He imagined it would probably, but he could not afford taking two years off with no income, nor was he eager to cough up $100,000 for another degree. Fortunately, he had already begun exploring an alternative to acquiring more business knowledge and skills. One evening, while clicking through business education opportunities on the Internet, he discovered MOOCs and a whole universe of people studying business on their own terms, without taking out a bank loan or leaving their jobs. Before joining that movement, he established his commitment by putting himself through the equivalent of a business school admissions process.

This chapter will help you figure out if a self-directed, MOOC-based business education will work for you. You begin by asking yourself some key questions: *Can I set aside sufficient time to study? Have I determined a specific goal I wish to achieve through independent study? Will I remain motivated to work hard in my self-directed program?*

Kristof and his wife spent many hours discussing his options. In the end, they agreed that Kristof would ask his boss to let him apply for an internal transfer. In a less stressful position, he could more easily find the time to study while remaining employed. While that would temporarily take him off the fast track to the top, he and his wife believed it would open up more possibilities in the future. His boss agreed to the transfer. After a few interviews, Kristof found a fit in the risk department, where the pace was much less frenetic. Best of all, he could almost walk to his new office.

Now, with a shorter commute and a more predictable schedule, he could dedicate a certain number of evenings and weekends to the effort. He did not know exactly what direction his online education would take, but he knew it would involve the world of economics and finance. As for motivation, Kristof had always been a self-starter who required little, if any, supervision when he set his sights on an ambitious goal.

Your own admissions test should mirror the admissions process of a traditional MBA program:

Step 1: Select yourself.

Step 2: Define your goals.

Step 3: Budget time and money.

Step 4: Hold yourself accountable.

As with everything in life, a successful outcome depends on careful preparation. Your self-administered admissions process will help prepare you for the adventure ahead. Imagine yourself as both a hopeful student, excited about the prospect of a career-launching business education, and as a hard-nosed admissions committee taking a clear-eyed look at a prospective student's ability to succeed. Put yourself behind the desk of an imaginary admissions officer and grill yourself about your suitability for self-directed study, the goals you wish to achieve, the budget of time and money you can afford, and your ability to keep working toward your goal, even when you're in a classroom of one, rather than a large lecture hall filled with other students.

Select Yourself

Before you enroll in any class, you must answer the first question a university admissions officer would ask: "Is this student prepared to succeed in the program being offered?" The answer, as it pertains to your self-directed business education, requires that you ask yourself this crucial question: "Am I capable of learning on my own?" Through my work with self-directed business learners, I have identified some common traits that the most successful ones share. Regardless of age, background, nationality, gender, or field of interest, they all possess an entrepreneurial spirit, a love of learning, and a professional attitude. Let's take a closer look at each of these essential traits.

Entrepreneurial. If you're reading this book, then you're already thinking like an entrepreneur. You want to take responsibility for your career and your future. You may not imagine yourself running your own business, but even if you work your whole life for a corporation, you approach problems with passion and creativity. Today, more than ever, employers in all fields, from healthcare and education to government and nonprofit work, value "intrapreneurs," employees who come up with innovative solutions to business problems. An entrepreneurial spirit will not only help you get ahead in whatever endeavor you pursue, it will help you remain firmly committed to your studies without direct supervision. Think about your previous or current schooling or employment. Do you prefer relying on your own intelligence and decisions, or would you rather follow orders and fulfill assignments given to you by others? If you put yourself in the former group, you may be an ideal candidate for a self-directed MBA equivalent. If not, you might fare better going the more traditional route to a business education.

Learning-oriented. Universally, those who succeed in self-directed studies love to learn. They value education in many forms, whether taking classes in a formal school setting or gaining new skills from a master or mentor. Whether young dogs or old dogs, they love learning new tricks. The psychologist Carol Dweck calls this a "growth mindset."[1] People with a growth mindset believe that they can always expand their talents, abilities, and intelligence.

Call it self-confidence or optimism or curiosity or belief in a better future, but it all boils down to the same trait—faith in one's ability to grow throughout one's entire life. Do you envision a better, more productive, more rewarding future for yourself, in terms of both personal fulfillment and financial well-being, or do you feel fairly content with your current situation? If you foresee a brighter future, you qualify for a self-directed business education. If not, you might more happily spend your spare time on something other than MOOCs and online learning.

Professional. You do not need a professional degree in medicine or law or business to think of yourself as a professional. Whether you are a sales rep or a systems analyst for a major bank, you simply need to take your work seriously. You care about making a difference in the world, and you aim to amplify your ability to make that difference. And, yes, you want to make more money. I have met stay-at-home moms who are using a self-directed business education to launch a business or get back into the workforce. And I have met gainfully employed engineers who are using the same kind of education to move higher up the corporate ladder. Do you take work seriously? Do you want to make more of a contribution to society? Would you like to make more money doing what you love to do? Then you're likely to do well in a self-directed business learning program.

Do you see yourself in the description above? Welcome to our ranks! In the world of self-directed learning, you will meet a lot of kindred spirits, people like our friend Kristof. His natural curiosity, drive, and willingness to take on new challenges have helped him to succeed, no matter where he worked in his organization.

Self-directed learners abound in all walks of life. Take my Uncle Dave, for example. Dave has spent his life farming corn, soy, and wheat in Missouri. On a recent visit to my uncle's farm, I came to appreciate the incredible entrepreneurialism, learning, and professionalism required of a successful farmer.

As we toured the grounds, Uncle Dave spoke eloquently and passionately about everything from plant science and chemistry to auto mechanics and electricity. The man knows how to fix a tractor, convert DC to AC current, and hedge prices on the international commodities market. As we strolled his property, he told me he was planning to drive to Iowa the next day to pick up a new piece of machinery called a "gravity table," a device that would help him recoup losses on a portion of his wheat harvest that had been damaged by heavy rains. Although he had never used such a machine, he knew he would figure it out. After all, Uncle Dave had always taught himself whatever he needed to know to make his farm a productive and profitable business. Hearing him talk about his business, I was blown away by my uncle, who often refers to himself as "a dumb farmer." Nothing could be further from the truth!

Now that you have joined Kristof and my Uncle Dave as a bona fide self-directed learner, you can take the next step—determining the results you want to achieve with your business education.

Define Your Goals

Every business school application contains a variation on this question: "Why do you want an MBA?" Before you begin your MBA journey, it's important to have a sense of the destination. For

Dorothy and her companions in *The Wizard of Oz*, the Emerald City and the all-powerful wizard provided a powerful incentive to keep moving forward. Of course, the power to achieve their goals lay inside them, not in the hands of a charlatan wizard. The same applies to your success in your business education; the keys to your success are inside you. As you travel down the path, you will need a strong incentive to stay the course, especially when your studies prove challenging.

For students in traditional business schools, the carrot of a degree, the stick of the grading system, and the fear of falling thousands of dollars into debt with nothing to show for it can supply powerful motivation. But you're on your own now. Only the power and pull of your goal can give you the courage you need to conquer the weariness and distractions that can and will pop up along your path.

Fortunately, whether or not you are currently able to articulate it, that goal is already inside of you. It's what inspired you to pick up this book in the first place. The purpose of this part of the admissions process is simply to define and document it, so that you can come back to it when you're bogged down in the details of balancing T-accounts or calculating the coefficient of variation for a supply chain forecast. Perhaps your big goal is already crystal clear in your mind. You may be able to say something as specific as, "My goal is to land a marketing job at a major book publisher," or, "My goal is to earn a promotion with my current company." If your big goal doesn't spring so easily to mind, consider these questions:

- What kind of work do you care about doing?
- What are the gaps in your training up to this point, and what do you hope will happen once you fill them?

- How do you plan or expect to use your business education?
- Is there a specific job you are hoping to get?
- Can a business education help you build the skills you need to start your own venture?
- What will your life look like after you complete your education?

Take Kristof, for example. He set a big goal, but he did not make it so minutely specific that it could hamper his quest. He knew he needed to stage a transition in his life, and he wanted to find a position that would draw on his expertise in economics, allow him to express his creative side, and provide enough work/life balance for him to spend time with his wife and daughters. That picture was clear and compelling enough to keep him motivated, even though he had not yet pinpointed a specific job title. You must be able to imagine yourself in the role and work environment that suit you best, even if you can't yet state it as specifically as "Vice President of Supply Chain Strategy for a major pharmaceutical company." It may also help to know that most independent business students begin their studies with a goal that falls into one of four major categories:

1. **The Executive.** You see yourself working as a manager. To do it well, you must acquire leadership and communication skills, at the very least. The Executive's goal involves becoming a stronger manager of individuals, teams, and processes. If you fall into this group, you may have already won a promotion from a technical role to one where you supervise the work of others. But a superior engineer does not necessarily make an

excellent manager. The same holds true for entrepreneurs. It takes one set of skills to launch a successful enterprise and quite another to manage more and more people.

2. **The Accelerator.** You want to move ever higher up the ladder. You're happy with your job and the company, but you want to grow with it, rising to ever-higher levels of responsibility. Major promotions will depend on you adding to your repertoire of skills, perhaps learning the art of persuasion and negotiation or learning the ins and outs of accounting, budgeting, and forecasting.

3. **The Entrepreneur.** You envision yourself starting or growing your own business. To succeed, you will need to know about a whole host of topics, from finance, accounting, and budgeting to marketing and sales. The Entrepreneur is a jack-of-all-trades and often a master of many. As the business grows, so does the Entrepreneur's set of skills.

4. **The Explorer.** You imagine a radical professional transformation. Such a change will require skills in many different business disciplines. A smorgasbord of courses may help the Explorer figure out where he or she best belongs in the business world. A self-directed business education can give you a taste of the whole spectrum of business specialties. It can also allow you to "test drive" your future without jumping right onto the fast track.

I'd like to make an important point here. One size shoe does not fit all feet; and all feet grow. At this very moment you may see two, three, or even all of these types in yourself. Or you may start out on an Executive path and, after gaining a lot of experience as a manager, decide to strike out on your own and start a new business. Your big goal should be flexible, allowing for your personal growth and a new direction dictated by changing circumstances. A stay-at-home dad decides to moonlight or, after his kids have gone off to college, go to work for a major corporation or expand his home-based business. A dentist may build a chain of dental offices then decide to sell the practice and take up jewelry making. Always keep in mind that a self-directed business education is a never-ending process. When you reach one mountaintop, another one pops up behind it. But here's the beautiful thing about this method of education. If you enroll in a traditional MBA program, switching gears can leave you deep in debt with no clear payoff from your sizable investment. In a self-made MBA program, you can go in an entirely different direction while incurring little or no cost beyond your own time and effort.

Try to paint a clear, big picture of your own imagined future. That vision can help keep you on the path when you get mired in the daily grind of studying and reading and learning. Once you're clear on your big goal, that idea that will motivate you to come back to your computer day after day, write it down and tape it above your workspace as a constant reminder. Once you feel comfortable with your goal, you can turn your attention to what can be the scariest parts of any MBA program: time and money.

Allocate the Right Amount of Time

Steve Jobs once said, "My favorite things in life don't cost any money. It's really clear that the most precious resource we all have is time."[2] As you go through your admissions process, consider that your time is just as valuable as your money, if not more so. If you are thinking seriously about diving into a self-directed business education, you are probably wrestling with a pretty full schedule already. With little room for added demands on your time, you must take a hard, honest look at your schedule. Can you make room for several hours a week to study online and read assigned material? Don't count on multitasking to accommodate a MOOC. You may be able to cook dinner listening to lectures on topics with which you are somewhat familiar, but you cannot possibly learn accounting or data analytics or financial valuation while tossing a Caesar salad or changing diapers or writing emails at work. You wouldn't pay $25,000 to a university for a semester and then attend only half of each class, unless you wouldn't mind pulling down Fs. Even though your self-administered MBA equivalent will cost you a lot less money, pretend that it will cost you as much as attending Stanford's business school. Your time is valuable. Invest it wisely, carving out $25,000 worth of space for your studies.

Budget at least four hours per week per course. A reasonable course load for a working person might be two courses at a time, or perhaps just one. When I first started studying business I could afford a fair amount of time because I was between jobs. I had the time to book a full schedule of four courses, which was practically as time-consuming as a full-time job. After I started working again, I could not afford to listen to lectures and do homework during the week, so I blocked off most of each Saturday for my studies.

I strongly advise that you build in time to pause and reflect. MBA students in traditional programs often complain that the harried pace of the MBA program leaves them with almost no time to relax and think. You need that reflective time to mull over what you're learning and put it all in perspective. Are you happy with your progress? Has the coursework been moving you closer to your goal? Can you determine the next course or set of courses that will move you in the right direction? Are you enjoying the experience? If you're not having fun, you'll not keep spending the right amount of time on your self-made MBA.

This may sound like strange advice from a coach, but I firmly believe that you embrace your education as a process of exploration and discovery. Prepare for surprises. Take time to look for them. You may find, as I did, that your studies take you in an entirely different direction than you had originally planned. I thought I wanted to boost my career in international development, and while that did indeed happen, I also discovered a previously unknown passion for entrepreneurship. You may start your business education with a goal that fits neatly into one of the four categories mentioned earlier (Executive, Accelerator, Entrepreneur, or Explorer), but as time goes by, you may find yourself shifting from one mode to another. Take time to reflect on that possibility.

Budget the Right Amount of Money

How much money should you invest in yourself and your future? Think of it as your scholarship fund. How and from whom you acquire it (money you have set aside for a rainy day, savings from your current salary, financial support from your employer, contributions from your family) matters less than the fact that you have earmarked a certain amount of money for your business education. Setting up this fund relieves you of anxiety if and when you need to pay for courses, materials, or experiences during your studies.

What kinds of expenses can you expect to incur during your business education? This short list includes most of the primary ones:

1. **MOOC certificates.** Most MOOCs on the big platforms, such as Coursera and edX, do not cost anything to audit. However, some providers of online business education require a fee for access to quizzes and assignments and for a certificate of completion. Typically these cost between $40 and $150. Setting aside some funds for certificates makes sense for a few reasons. First, they offer proof of your perseverance and professionalism. A certificate proves that you are a determined go-getter who will invest time and money acquiring business acumen. Second, they strengthen your determination because they provide motivation to stay the course. Behavioral economists call it "loss aversion." It turns out that we dislike losing even more than we enjoy winning. Hence, we will more likely complete a course that we've paid for than one that didn't cost us a nickel. Third, it can serve as a tangible reminder that you are making progress toward your goals.

2. **Specialized content.** While you can take many courses without dipping into your scholarship fund, some providers do charge fees for courses. Often, skills-focused courses taught by industry experts are available only to fee-paying students. The fees can range from under $10 to over $1,000. You will probably want to invest in such courses as you progress with your business education and begin to concentrate your time and resources on the area of expertise you want to develop.

3. **Books.** Most courses assign required reading or suggest supplemental books on the subject. Usually, these readings are provided as downloadable documents and are included with the course. The good news is that most MOOCs do not require you to purchase pricey textbooks, which can cost over $100 apiece. However, you would be wise to supplement your classroom

education with books. Imagine that you are building a business library that not only gives you immediate knowledge but also allows you to refresh your learning later in your career.

4. **Coaching, mentorship, and networking.** We will spend much more time throughout this book discussing how to replicate the in-person components of a business education. For now, suffice it to say that coaches, mentors, and a strong professional network can play a major role in the development of your career. These services can add a significant amount of money to the cost of a self-directed business education. For example, the services of an executive coach can run over $150 per hour. Use such resources sparingly, perhaps setting aside $500 for coaching, networking, and mentoring services.

5. **Travel.** Travel, particularly international travel, can give students in traditional business school programs a valuable global perspective. Of course, international travel can cost a pretty penny. Consider the business benefits of any trip you take to a foreign country. Planning a surfing adventure in Costa Rica? Combine it with a few weeks helping young Costa Rican entrepreneurs develop their business plans. If you decide to include international travel in your curriculum you will need to beef up your scholarship fund by at least $3,000 to cover airfare, accommodations, and meals during your international experience. We will look more closely at the benefits of international travel in Chapter 9.

When determining how much money you want to bank in your scholarship account, you might ask yourself this central question: *How much money am I willing to spend on opening up a whole new world of career opportunities?* You can spend your money a lot of different ways. What will you get out of a given expenditure? You might yearn for a lavish dinner at an expensive restaurant, a new pair of designer jeans, or a weekend getaway at a mountain resort, but spending money on those indulgences will not give you many long-term benefits. A self-directed business education will. It can add many thousands of dollars to your lifetime earning potential. When budgeting for your business education, never forget to ask yourself, "What can I hope for in terms of a return on my investment?" Every good business decision aims at a good ROI.

You can use My Business Education Budget worksheet (Figure 1-1) to help focus your thinking about your own scholarship fund.

Figure 1-1. **My Business Education Budget**

TYPE OF EXPENSE	COST PER UNIT	NUMBER OF UNITS	TOTAL
Course certificates	$40–$150		
Specialized content	$10–$1,000		
Books	$15–$25		
Professional coaching, mentorship, and networking	$500–$1,500		
Travel	$3,000–$6,000		
		Total budget:	

Hold Yourself Accountable

You stand to reap an enormous windfall from your business education, getting a much higher return on your investment than a graduate from a top business school since your education comes at a fraction of the cost. It all depends on holding yourself accountable for the result. The going will get tough at times. Other demands on your time, family commitments, dwindling resources, frustration, and just plain weariness can threaten your progress. When that happens (and it will happen, trust me), you need to muster support from within and from your network of friends, family, and fellow students.

To maintain your momentum, you might try a few of these tactics:

- Put some skin in the game. Regardless of the size of your financial investment in your education, you do not want to lose that investment. Only continued hard work can make it pay off.
- Tell friends, family, and coworkers about your plans. They can offer much-needed encouragement along the way.
- Use one of the many goal-setting apps available for smart-phones and tablets. Apps such as Way of Life and Coach.me will send you daily reminders, track your progress toward your goals, and help you manage your time.
- Discuss your educational plans with your supervisor at work. Your employer will value your effort, provided it doesn't interfere with your work.
- Acquire an accountability partner, someone who can serve as a weekly or monthly progress monitor. Regular feedback can help keep you on track.
- Enlist the help of a career coach. A coach can help you clarify your values and your goals, making it easier to stay motivated to reach them.
- Join or create a business study group. We will explore this topic at length in Chapter 6, but for now, think about

finding a few teammates who can lend you a helping hand or a sympathetic shoulder when you need it.

You've set up a scholarship fund. You've devised ways to maintain your motivation. You have taken your destiny into your own hands. Now you are ready to complete your first *Adviser's Challenge*. These hands-on activities, often involving problem solving or project-based learning, encourage you to take an active approach to your education. The first one (see Figure 1-2) asks you to lay the groundwork for your success in your business education, taking into account the insights you've gained through your self-administered admissions process.

Figure 1-2

▶ ADVISER'S CHALLENGE ◀

LAY THE GROUNDWORK FOR SUCCESS

❏ **Prepare your study space.** Create a comfortable, quiet study environment where you can spend time without distractions and interruptions. Working on your laptop in the living room while others are watching a football game can stall your progress.

❏ **Ask others to respect your quiet time.** Be sure to ask your roommates, family, and friends to honor your need for stretches of time when you must concentrate on your studies. They will appreciate knowing when you will be available again.

❏ **Set a study schedule.** Designate particular days and times as dedicated study periods. A preplanned schedule helps you form good study habits. Choose times for study when you feel fresh and eager to work. As a weekend or evening student, you may struggle to find times where you can get the most from your studies. Tired people do not make the best learners. Once you've chosen your study times, mark them on your calendar.

☐ **Reward your own efforts.** Periodically treat yourself, even if it's something small, like a chocolate bar or a new book. These rewards can provide excellent incentives to keep on keeping on. As you begin your education, plan what events will trigger such rewards, whether that's finishing a course, getting a good grade on a test, or completing an Adviser's Challenge.

☐ **Notify an accountability partner or partners.** Let the supporters in your network know that you're embarking on a new educational adventure. Make sure they also know when to expect status updates from you. The more your network knows about your progress, the more support you will receive. You do not want to disappoint your best advocates any more than you want to disappoint yourself.

☐ **Make a contract with yourself.** Write down your motivation and accountability plan. A monthly or quarterly review of this document can remind you about your goals and your strategy for reaching them.

How does the admissions process work in practice? Here is how it worked for Hillary, a young woman who had always dreamed of starting her own publishing business. A passionate lover of books and storytelling, she envisioned a business that would combine literature with her deep commitment to social justice. But she knew that motivation alone would not make her dream come true. She needed some serious business training to get her new venture off the ground.

Hillary had already discovered MOOCs. She was enjoying a course on gamification, a popular concept in education design, when she stumbled across my No-Pay MBA blog and saw that I was recruiting people to join a learning group, a network whose members would support one another's self-directed efforts. As she contemplated taking the plunge into business MOOCs and joining a cohort of other learners, Hillary pondered her past experience with self-directed learning. She loved the MOOC she was taking and she could easily picture herself succeeding in almost any course, as long as she found it interesting and knew it could help her advance her career as a budding entrepreneur. Of course, given her goal of starting a business, she fell squarely into the Entrepreneur camp.

What about the time and money it would take to reach her goals? At the time, Hillary was a single parent, caring for an infant daughter. She decided she could find time for her studies while her daughter napped. Nap times might fluctuate, but Hillary would always have sufficient time to take at least one new course. Like most single moms, she was living on a pretty tight budget, but she figured out a way to set aside $250 to finance her studies.

Finally, to hold herself accountable, Hillary did join the No-Pay MBA learning cohort. Her father gave her his unquestioning support, and she did manage to complete most of her studies during nap times. Most important, perhaps, she developed strong relationships both with other MOOC MBA students and with a group of women entrepreneurs, all of whom offered tremendous support, especially when Hillary felt rather worn out, as every single mom does from time to time. In the end, her self-directed, debt-free business education has paid tremendous dividends. Her coursework provided exactly the information Hillary needed to launch her business, giving her the confidence and the methods to get a business off the ground without seeking venture financing. The social-impact-focused, multimedia publishing house she now runs enjoys a steadily growing client list. Hillary's self-directed learning and entrepreneurial spirit also landed her a speaking role at the 2017 Women's Economic Forum, an opportunity that stemmed directly from the networking Hillary did as part of her education. You'll be hearing more about Hillary and her inspiring story in the chapters to come.

Have you completed your self-administered admissions application? If so, you're ready to dive in and start learning! Your first task will be to build a foundational understanding of business concepts and start learning to speak the language of business.

POINTS TO REMEMBER

1. Conduct your own admissions process in which you select yourself, set a big goal, budget time and money, and hold yourself accountable.
2. Identify yourself as an entrepreneurial learning-oriented professional.
3. Determine your specific goal and consider whether you are an Executive, an Accelerator, an Entrepreneur, or an Explorer.
4. Set aside the right amount of time and money for your studies.
5. Write a concrete plan for holding yourself accountable for results.
6. Use the admissions process as a time for reflection, making sure to build other such moments into your overall business education.

2

Meet the Modern MOOC

Attending Your Virtual Orientation

BEFORE you go any further, you might want to attend the equivalent of freshman orientation. If you already know how MOOCs operate, you can skip this little chapter. If not, spend a few minutes reading the following pages. They will give you a satellite's-eye view of the terrain ahead.

Massive open online courses, or MOOCs, burst into public consciousness between 2011 and 2012, inspiring *The New York Times* to declare 2012 "The Year of the MOOC."[1] Yet online education did not appear because someone coined the term MOOC. From the very beginning, the Internet offered a way for people, initially scientists, to learn from others and share information around the world. So what makes this new breed of online courses so special? In the early 2000s some of the top universities, including prestigious institutions such as MIT, Yale, and Stanford, began experimenting with offering portions of their curricula for free online. MIT, for example, began its OpenCourseWare project in 2001 with the expressed goal of making all graduate and undergraduate courses available at no cost online. But, like any new form of electronic social communication, early forays into open courses looked like horse-and-buggy travel compared to today's high-speed trains and tomorrow's starships (a topic we'll discuss in Chapter 9). Back then, you could obtain the syllabus for a course, links to some reading materials, and a few poor-quality recorded lectures. In some cases you could even get instructions to complete a few assignments. But the experience lacked interactivity and graded assessments. Nor could you synchronize your experience with other learners. You might be simultaneously using course materials with 1,000 fellow students, but you could not connect with them.

By the late-2000s, several professors and teams of professors in different parts of North America set about building courses that took full advantage of the digital age, replicating (as much as possible) a lively and engaging classroom anyone, anywhere could join. Stanford University's computer science department jumped enthusiastically into the fray. Beginning in 2008, computer science professor Andrew Ng put ten of Stanford's most popular engineering courses online for use by the public. Meanwhile, his colleague Daphne Koller started experimenting with the "flipped classroom" model as a way of boosting student learning. The flipped classroom involved recording and distributing lectures with quizzes embedded in them for students to watch before class, while making physical attendance optional. In-person class time was used for working through problem sets and other hands-on activities, not for passively listening to lectures. Meanwhile, around the same time, a group of academics in Canada were experimenting with a course structure in which a small group of tuition-paying students studied online with a much larger group of nonpaying students. This group of pioneers coined the term "massive open online course," or "MOOC."[2]

However, one course really put MOOCs on the map: *Introduction to AI*, created by Stanford professors Peter Norvig and Sebastian Thrun, two of the world's best-known artificial intelligence experts. In 2011, Norvig, a former NASA scientist, and Thrun, renowned for his work on self-driving cars, released a graduate-level course on artificial intelligence that was open to anyone who wanted to take it. As soon as the course was announced, it attracted 58,000 registrants from 175 countries, even before going live.[3] When the course began, students from around the world flooded onto the platform to stream video lectures, puzzle over problem sets, and answer one another's questions in a discussion forum. Word spread, and learners continued to join the course week by week until a whopping 160,000 people had taken part in it. The course professors were stunned by the response to *Introduction to AI.* After Thrun and Norvig's course went massive, other courses soon followed. Andrew Ng and Daphne Koller joined forces to offer courses on a platform designed by Ng and some of his students. That platform would evolve into Coursera, the largest and most well-known MOOC platform.[4] Each of their first courses attracted around 100,000 students.

Following the success of these initial experiments, the next year saw MOOCs blast into the stratosphere. Thrun and Norvig's partnership became the MOOC platform Udacity, joining Koller and Ng's Coursera. A third platform, a nonprofit called edX, grew out of a collaboration between Harvard and MIT. Based on the overwhelming response to their pilot offerings, these three platforms, sometimes referred to in the early days of MOOCs as "the Big Three," set about making first-rate educational experiences on every subject imaginable, at little or no cost. Students from Singapore to San Francisco could study creative writing or computer science with the click of a mouse.

Now you can log in from anywhere, register for a free account, and within minutes you can be attending lectures, taking quizzes, submitting assignments, and engaging in spirited exchange in a discussion forum. Eager learners, from precocious high school students to Ph.D. candidates and retirees, have flocked to MOOCs as the most Ph.D. efficient, least expensive, and most flexible way to get a top-notch education. In 2015 Coursera, which has become the largest MOOC platform, boasted more than 17 million students. Students had their pick of over 4,000 individual courses, and the numbers are still rising.[5] In addition to the original Big Three, platforms such as FutureLearn, NovoEd, Iversity, MiriadaX, and Open2Study all offer courses for learners around the world. Universities from the United States, Europe, and many other parts of the world have partnered with these providers to offer their courses to a global audience.

If you are a MOOC freshman, you should know how the basic learning format works. A typical MOOC consists of a variety of learning modules, including recorded lectures, quizzes, written assignments, and problem sets. Many MOOCs offer links to supplemental reading assignments. Most include a discussion forum where students can interact. Some MOOCs run on a set schedule with a defined start and end date and assignments due on a weekly basis. Increasingly, however, MOOC providers have been shifting toward a "self-paced" model in which students work through the course modules and assignments when they can find time and at their own pace.

Costs vary across the various MOOC platforms, but the majority of them operate on a "freemium" model. It costs nothing to register for a course and to participate in some or most of the modules. Students who wish to earn a certificate and, in the case of Coursera, to access all quizzes and assignments must pay a relatively modest fee. Throughout this book, I use the word MOOC as a general term to refer to online courses that are open to the public and do not require enrollment in a credit-bearing degree program.

Coursera and edX embody the classic MOOC model, with most courses produced by universities to match their on-campus offerings. Udacity, once the third member of the Big Three MOOC providers, has shifted away from the academic model and now offers a set of technology-based "nanodegrees" designed to prepare people for technical careers. A third model comes from platforms such as Lynda and Udemy, which function as open marketplaces for courses. On such platforms, industry experts sell short courses at a range of prices. For our purposes, I will refer to all of these online courses as MOOCs.

If you've never taken a MOOC before, now is the perfect time to get started. You'll take plenty of business-related MOOCs throughout your quest for a top-notch business education, but for your first course I recommend one of the most popular MOOCs of all time, because it applies to all kinds of learning. That course is *Learning How to Learn*, taught by Barbara Oakley and Terry Sejnowski of the University of California at San Diego. The course draws on research from the field of neuroscience in order to teach you how to become a better learner, no matter what you are studying. The professors who created the course used state-of-the-art pedagogic techniques to create a student experience that captures and holds your attention while imparting valuable knowledge. The course boasts a global fan base, many of whom give it credit for helping them succeed in learning everything from computer coding to Chinese. To register for the course, simply visit www.Coursera.org, type "learning how to learn" into the search bar, click "enroll," and sign up for your free account. Voilà! You've started your first MOOC.

POINTS TO REMEMBER

1. Underscore the validity of a MOOC-based MBA by delving deeper into the history of online education.
2. Visit the Appendices at the back of the book and explore some of the wonderful learning opportunities in the MOOC universe.
3. Familiarize yourself with the typical MOOC learning formats by researching some of the courses you plan to take.
4. Consider taking *Learning How to Learn*, offered by the University of California at San Diego on the Coursera platform.

3

Lay Your Foundation

Learning to Speak
the Language of Business

MICHAEL had been working at Brady Books, a college text-book publisher, for two years as a sales rep, when the company promoted him to an editorial position. Having majored in English in college, he was looking forward to using the skills he'd acquired at school in his new role, and he hoped that a successful record as an editor would quickly boost him into a management position. Further success, he knew, would depend on learning the business side of publishing. Toward that end, he arranged a lunch date with one of the company's senior accountants, the national sales manager, and his boss, the firm's executive editor. As he listened to the three men chat, he felt as if he had stumbled into a *Star Wars* bar where everyone was speaking incomprehensible gibberish.

"The ROI last quarter was way off target," muttered the accountant.

"I thought we were measuring ROIC now," countered the sales manager. "Anyway, we'll turn it around with our new USP."

Michael's boss shook his head. "We need to tear down the silos, so all stakeholders can get on the same page."

"Yes, cross-functional teams. That's the ticket."

The accountant took a deep breath. "But we need to outsource more in-house work and think strategically about supply chain management. And don't forget our Six Sigma initiative and our move to JIT inventory."

Michael's head was spinning. "Do I need to go back to school and learn business as a second language just to talk with these guys?"

Professionals in the business world do speak their own language, and the traditional B-school curriculum delivers a good deal of vocabulary. While no business student could possibly master all the specialized terms and acronyms from every discipline, by the time they graduate, students have become quite comfortable speaking the language of business. As you begin your independent business studies, you should aim to gain fluency as well, so you won't shake your head in confusion, as Michael did, when speaking with business professionals who toss around terms like ROI, MVP, market segmentation, cost of capital, "lean," Six Sigma, and hundreds of others. The more articulate you become with business as a second language, and the more fully you understand the concepts behind the words, the more confident you will feel engaging with the business world.

Start with the Foundation

You may have taken a few MOOCs already, or you may be just entering the world of nontraditional business studies. Whether you are a veteran of self-directed learning or a newbie, think of every MOOC you take not only as a source of knowledge, but also as a language lab. Thirty years ago, before the dawn of the Internet, Michael would have learned business terminology by subscribing to business-oriented newspapers like *The Wall Street Journal* and reading classic business books such as Peter Drucker's *The Effective*

Executive. These days, you have an advantage. Instead of picking up business terminology here and there, through this article or that popular business book, you can take a systematic approach, enrolling in MOOCs that correspond directly to the core courses at such top business schools as Harvard, Stanford, and Wharton.

For a moment, I'd like you to imagine your business education as a pyramid. At the base of the pyramid you set a broad, solid foundation. Each brick in that foundation represents a set of core business concepts, such as unique selling proposition and customer value (marketing); return on investment and amortization (finance); and project scope and performance ratings (management). The second, slightly narrower layer of the pyramid includes the general business skills all business professionals need to know, such as giving a presentation, conducting a negotiation, and reading a balance sheet. The third, even narrower layer consists of specific skills that pertain to a particular business discipline. An accountant needs to work magic with an Excel spreadsheet; a sales manager should understand a wide range of selling techniques; a general manager must know how to conduct annual reviews and inspire her team to perform. Finally, at the top of the pyramid sit the hands-on, practical experiences seldom offered in a classroom setting, skills you can only learn in the real world. Our friend Michael, for example, got most of his business education on the job, acquiring authors, editing manuscripts, and supervising junior editors. "There's business school," he says, "then there's the School of Hard-Won Experience. You never graduate from *that* school. Just when you think you know everything and have seen it all, something brand-new and unexpected takes you by surprise."

Traditional business schools provide the foundation by requiring students to take a set of core courses during their first year in the program. A 2010 survey of 886 MBA programs found that almost all of them (85 percent) required courses on the following topics: accounting, marketing, finance, management, and economics.[1] Many, but not all, required coursework in communication, ethics, supply chain management, change management, and negotiation. Depending on your prior experience and training, you may have already laid many of the bricks in your foundation. You may also have added a number of skills and experiences to the structure. In Chapter 1, we discussed setting goals for your business education. Depending on your specific goals, you may decide to concentrate more of your energy on a particular layer in your pyramid. For example, you may have years of experience as a salesperson, but now you've been made sales manager. Like all students of business, you will want to start with the foundation, making sure your understanding of core business concepts is complete. Then, you might focus on learning managerial skills and using them on the job right away, building the top layer of your pyramid simultaneously with the middle layers. In a traditional B-school setting you would build the pyramid from the ground up. In a self-directed program, you may assemble it like you would a jigsaw puzzle, depending on your shifting needs. In the end, however, you want to have assembled a solid and complete Mastery Pyramid (see Figure 3-1) that can support your career growth.

Select Your Core Curriculum

One of the most beloved MOOCs among the business learners in my community is *Introduction to Financial Accounting*, taught by Professor Brian Bushee of the University of Pennsylvania's

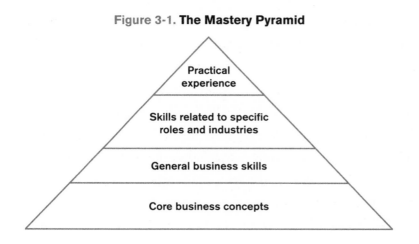

Figure 3-1. **The Mastery Pyramid**

Practical experience

Skills related to specific roles and industries

General business skills

Core business concepts

Wharton School of Business and offered on the Coursera platform. Despite its rather dry title, the course offers a delightfully engaging approach to the subject. A gifted teacher, Professor Bushee brings accounting to life with highly practical exercises and amusing interludes in which a cast of cartoon students makes wisecracks and asks humorous questions. The very first video lecture of the course begins with four cartoon characters standing in an airport lounge. One, a professionally dressed woman, opens a conversation by saying to the other three, "Hi, what's up?"

One of the other characters answers her in Swedish. Another responds in Esperanto. The third answers in the language of accounting. "I am excited because my company took a noncash, nonrecurring provision for impairment of goodwill, and now we'll have lower amortization expenses and deferred tax assets in the future," he says.

"Doesn't anyone speak English here?" asks the frustrated first character.

Professor Bushee then appears on the screen to describe financial accounting as "the language of business." The course, he promises, will teach you to read a balance sheet, conduct simple financial analyses, and speak knowledgeably with people who use financial jargon. Financial accounting makes sense as a first course in a core curriculum because it imparts so many words essential to a strong business vocabulary. Bushee's course is part of the Wharton Business Foundations Specialization, a set of four courses drawn from the school's first-year curriculum: financial accounting, marketing, operations management, and corporate finance. Since you are setting up your own private business school, you can and should structure its core curriculum according to your unique situation, background, goals, experience, and skills. You can reinvent the wheel to suit your specific purposes, or you can emulate Wharton's (or the one required by any other top B-school).

However you go about it, you should include certain subjects in your core curriculum. To assemble your own core curriculum, you can draw them from this list of foundational subjects:

- **Business Ethics:** how to apply ethics and value-based decision making in a business environment
- **Business Leadership:** how to establish a vision and motivate others to realize it in a business setting
- **Corporate Finance:** how to make decisions about borrowing, raising, and investing money
- **Entrepreneurship:** how to start and sustain a new business venture
- **Financial Accounting:** how to keep track of and report on the money that comes into and goes out of a business
- **Marketing:** how to create and deliver value for customers
- **Microeconomics:** how to analyze the behavior of firms and individuals within markets

- **Project Management:** how to achieve a one-time, nonrepeating set of business objectives
- **Operations Management:** how to improve efficiency in repeating processes within a business

Customize Your Core Curriculum

At this point you may be thinking to yourself, "Hold on. This list seems incomplete. My friend who recently got an MBA from the Tuck School studied Change Management during his very first semester." Indeed, the list could include many other subjects. If Change Management or Self-Directed Teams excites you, feel free to add one or more of those topics to your core curriculum. Your customized set of core courses should reflect your background, experience, interests, and needs. If you dream of working in supply chain management, for example, you will surely want to include at least one course on that topic in your core course list.

Consider writing a mission statement for your business education then choosing a core curriculum that will fulfill that mission. Traditional schools require many of the same courses, but each one has developed its own brand identity. For example, Yale sets itself apart from its competitors by emphasizing global leadership and the softer, people-oriented side of business: "Whatever your leadership ambitions, you need to understand how markets work and how to build a thriving organization. But to make a deep impact in coming decades, you also need to be able to navigate the complexity that exists where sectors, regions, and cultures intersect in an increasingly connected world."[2]

MIT's Sloan School of Management, on the other hand, proclaims itself as a center for innovative thinking: "MIT Sloan is about invention. It's about ideas that are made to matter. At MIT Sloan, we discover tomorrow's interesting and important challenges and opportunities. We go where we want to have impact. And then, we invent the future."[3]

Whatever core curriculum you tailor to reflect your personal brand, you should consider the fact that most schools include three major categories of study: Quantitative and Financial Analysis, Management and Leadership, and Big-Picture Thinking. As you choose your four to six foundational subjects, aim to distribute your choices over these three areas, selecting one or two subjects from each.

In the Quantitative and Financial Analysis part of the curriculum, you will find topics such as finance and accounting, data analysis, and economics. Successful businesspeople know their way around budgets, balance sheets, and customer data. Wharton enjoys a reputation for imparting wisdom in those areas. Management and Leadership centers on people skills and includes such topics as human resources management, project management, operations management, and management theory, motivation, and team building. That's Yale's brand. Finally, as MIT's mission states, tomorrow's business leaders need to think big, chart new courses, and innovate new products and services in the marketplace. Big-Picture Thinking courses cover topics such as marketing, entrepreneurship, and business strategy. Your success in whatever business field or function you choose will probably involve skills from all three categories.

Let's see how one student customized her core curriculum according to her personal goals and career direction. Louisa works in

Product and Customer Strategy at a Cincinnati tech startup called LISNR (pronounced "listener"). She relishes the job's fast pace and the fact that new challenges come across her desk practically every day. But since this young performing-arts major did not take a single business course in college, she needs to learn the business terminology that will enable her to communicate effectively with people in sales meetings to strategy sessions.

Before Louisa took this new job, she had begun to hone her business acumen during a stint as a contractor for Procter & Gamble and through several entrepreneurial moonlighting projects, including cofounding a nonprofit organization. When she landed her job with LISNR, she decided to take a more systematic approach to acquiring a business education. When planning her first set of classes in her self-directed program, Louisa chose to begin with two subjects that would introduce her to entirely new ideas: Professor Bushee's renowned *Introduction to Financial Accounting* (offered by Coursera) and *How to Build a Startup* (taught by Silicon Valley entrepreneur Steve Blank on the Udacity platform). Like many liberal arts majors, Louisa found accounting challenging. However, she soldiered through it and later found the knowledge she had gained extremely useful on the job. For example, Louisa's position as an account manager involves interacting with prospective clients, often over meals or in social settings. Having studied accounting, Louisa could now see the importance of meticulously tracking the expenses involved with such client meetings and outings. The company's profitability depends on controlling all of the costs associated with closing a sale.

Louisa's second choice made a lot of sense. Not every business student would include entrepreneurship as a core course, but

Louisa has always fancied herself as having entrepreneurial qualities and currently works for a startup. She also runs a small career coaching business in her off-hours and dreams of founding her own tech company one day. In *How to Build a Startup* Louisa learned the way entrepreneurs must think about their new ventures, adopting a perspective much different from those who work for and manage mature businesses. "Working in a startup, I used to get really frustrated when whatever I was doing wasn't working," she says. "Now I can see that I'm not trying to operate a well-oiled corporate machine. I'm trying to research, learn, iterate, and pivot if necessary." The course not only gave her knowledge and a new perspective, it taught her the language she needs to think and talk about the subject.

Her core curriculum propelled Louisa toward her goals. As you customize yours, keep your goals firmly in mind. If, like Louisa, you are an Entrepreneur, interested in working in a startup and/or starting your own venture, you will surely want to include a course on entrepreneurship in your early studies. If you are an Executive, looking to become a more effective manager, you will undoubtedly select one or two management courses. An Accelerator, seeking to amass technical skills, might want to include a more specialized subject such as data analysis, for example, or digital marketing among his or her foundational courses. Finally, if you see yourself as an Explorer, yearning to broaden your horizons and possibly make a big career change, then you should study as widely as you can, seeking out unfamiliar topics that will offer you a fresh perspective on the world of work.

The sample core curricula in Figure 3-2 can get you started. Of course, you will design your own curriculum to suit your particular goals and needs.

Figure 3-2. **Sample Core Curricula**

	EXECUTIVE	ACCELERATOR	EXPLORER	ENTREPRENEUR
Quantitative and Financial Analysis	1. Financial Accounting (e.g., *Introduction to Financial Accounting*)	1. Corporate Finance (e.g., *Introduction to Corporate Finance*)	1. Microeconomics	1. Financial Accounting (e.g., *Introduction to Financial Accounting*)
	2. Corporate Finance (e.g., *Introduction to Corporate Finance*)	2. Data Analysis (e.g., *The Data Scientist's Toolbox*)	2. Corporate Finance (e.g., *Introduction to Corporate Finance*)	
Management and Leadership	3. Business Ethics (e.g., *New Models of Business in Society*)	3. Project Management (e.g., *Fundamentals of Project Planning and Management*)	3. Business Ethics (e.g., *New Models of Business in Society*)	2. Project Management (e.g., *Fundamentals of Project Planning and Management*)
	4. Business Leadership (e.g., *Foundations of Everyday Leadership*)		4. Operations Management (e.g., *Introduction to Operations Management*)	
Big-Picture Thinking	5. Marketing (e.g., *Introduction to Marketing*)	4. Entrepreneurship (e.g., *How to Build a Startup*)	5. Entrepreneurship (e.g., *How to Build a Startup*)	3. Entrepreneurship (e.g., *How to Build a Startup*)
			6. Marketing (e.g., *Introduction to Marketing*)	4. Marketing (e.g., *Introduction to Marketing*)

Use the template in Figure 3-3 to record your core curriculum for future reference.

Figure 3-3. My Core Curriculum

Quantitative and Financial Analysis topics:

1. _____

2. _____

3. _____

4. _____

Management and Leadership topics:

1. _____

2. _____

3. _____

4. _____

Big-Picture Thinking topics:

1. _____

2. _____

3. _____

4. _____

Choose Your First Courses

Now that you've selected the topics for your core curriculum, you want to zero in on your first set of courses. Search the major platforms or consult the list of suggested courses at the end of this book (Appendix A), and select a MOOC that corresponds to each topic you plan to study as you learn the language of business. Keep in mind that providers create new courses all the time. My list may be a helpful starting place, but you will also want to make sure you aren't missing any gems that have come online since this book was written.

All of the online platforms listed here offer business courses. Each one also contains a search function; just type in a keyword ("marketing," for example), then note the courses that pertain to your topic.

ACADEMIC MOOC PLATFORMS

- Coursera.org—the biggest and best-known MOOC provider, with the best selection of business MOOCs
- EdX.org—the second biggest MOOC provider, started as a nonprofit collaboration between Harvard and MIT, also with a good selection of business courses
- NovoEd.org—beloved by many for its group-oriented courses, including many courses on entrepreneurship and the social sector
- FutureLearn.com—includes a very good set of short, business-focused courses from British universities
- Iversity.org—a European MOOC platform offering many courses in German and some offerings in English, particularly in entrepreneurship

- MiriadaX.net—offering university courses, including business courses, in Spanish
- Open2Study.com—an Australian platform offering free courses and accredited degrees from Open Universities Australia

OTHER LEARNING PLATFORMS

- ALISON.com—free, skills-focused courses including certificates, on a platform that operates well even without a high-speed Internet connection
- Canvas.net—offers a variety of free business courses, many on specialized topics
- KhanAcademy.org—a free tutoring site aimed at high school and early college students, with some helpful materials on finance and economics
- Learning.ly—platform managed by The Economist Group that sells courses by authors, academics, and industry experts
- Lynda.com—fee-based courses on professional topics, often focused on specific skills
- Udacity.com—one of the original MOOC platforms that now offers technology-focused "nanodegree" programs, with strong offerings in technology entrepreneurship
- Udemy.com—offers a wide selection of courses taught by industry professionals, many focusing on concrete skills

Another way of finding courses is to browse a MOOC search engine. For example, Class Central (http://www.Class-Central.

com) pulls together the offerings from many different platforms and in a variety of different languages. The site also hosts a ratings system, where students can leave reviews of courses they have taken. Dhawal Shah, the founder of Class Central, created the site after embarking on his own MOOC adventure. Upon completing a master's degree in Computer Science from Georgia Tech, Dhawal was looking for ways to keep expanding his repertoire of skills and land a job with a Silicon Valley tech startup. He began his journey at the dawn of the MOOC era by enrolling in *Introduction to AI*. Amazed at the quality of instruction, Dhawal quickly became a MOOC enthusiast. Back then, he says, "Coursera hadn't gotten the name Coursera, Udacity hadn't gotten the name Udacity. These were just Stanford online courses, all on different websites. So I created a one-page site to track all of them." Although it began as a side project that would demonstrate Dhawal's programming skills, Class Central quickly took on a life of its own as more and more people used it to find and review online courses. As Dhawal's skills increased, he greatly enhanced the functionality of the site. As of this writing, it had become the world's number-one search engine for finding open courses.

As you select the business courses you will take, you can record them in a spreadsheet like the one in Figure 3-4.

At this point, you are ready to start studying! The Adviser's Challenge in Figure 3-5 is your step-by-step guide to getting started on your first set of courses.

Figure 3-4. **Business Courses That I Plan to Take**

QUANTITATIVE AND FINANCIAL ANALYSIS COURSES				
Subject	Courses	Platform	Start date	End date
MANAGEMENT AND LEADERSHIP COURSES				
Subject	Courses	Platform	Start date	End date
BIG-PICTURE THINKING COURSES				
Subject	Courses	Platform	Start date	End date

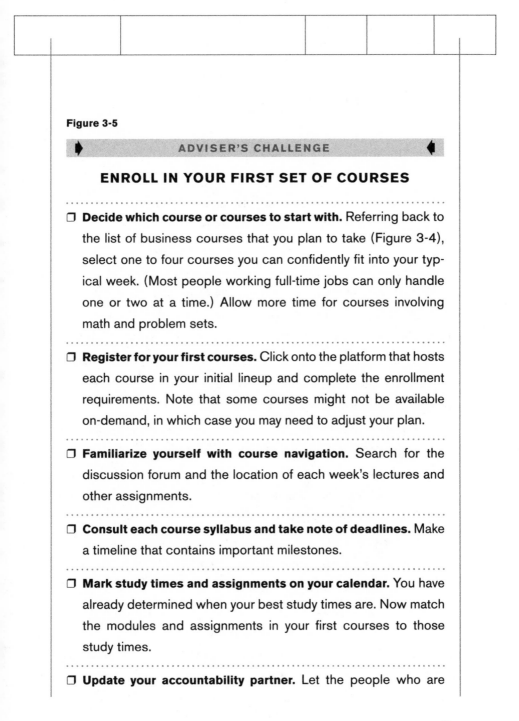

Figure 3-5

► ADVISER'S CHALLENGE ◄

ENROLL IN YOUR FIRST SET OF COURSES

❐ **Decide which course or courses to start with.** Referring back to the list of business courses that you plan to take (Figure 3-4), select one to four courses you can confidently fit into your typical week. (Most people working full-time jobs can only handle one or two at a time.) Allow more time for courses involving math and problem sets.

❐ **Register for your first courses.** Click onto the platform that hosts each course in your initial lineup and complete the enrollment requirements. Note that some courses might not be available on-demand, in which case you may need to adjust your plan.

❐ **Familiarize yourself with course navigation.** Search for the discussion forum and the location of each week's lectures and other assignments.

❐ **Consult each course syllabus and take note of deadlines.** Make a timeline that contains important milestones.

❐ **Mark study times and assignments on your calendar.** You have already determined when your best study times are. Now match the modules and assignments in your first courses to those study times.

❐ **Update your accountability partner.** Let the people who are following your education know that you have registered for your first set of courses.

· ·

☐ **Complete the introductory module of one or more courses.** Get ready, get set, go!

Immerse Yourself in the Language and Culture of Business

When choosing your courses, you need not limit yourself to my suggestions, or even to academic MOOCs. Your self-made MBA can include books and videos and even an occasional class at a brick-and-mortar school. For example, Michael, the English major who needed to go "back to school" to acquire the business language he needed to succeed in book publishing, asked his boss for a list of books that would provide a good starting point. He read Peter Drucker's *The Effective Executive* and Douglas McGregor's *The Human Side of Business*. When he became a business book editor, he learned a lot from the manuscripts he read. He also picked the brains of the professors he met on the job. "Today, I'd take several MOOCS," he says. "And I'd look for relevant YouTube videos. I would still find a mentor, like my old boss, who could advise me on ways I could immerse myself in the culture of business."

In addition to taking courses in accounting, finance, marketing, and other fields, you should look for non-classroom sources of knowledge. Suppose you wanted to learn to speak French. You could take four years of language classes in college, but nothing would help you become more fluent than living for a year in Paris. A new language does not just involve words and phrases; it functions within the context of a culture. You're not learning the language of business for the fun of it but to apply it in a real-world business setting.

When I joined the Peace Corps in 2009, I already spoke fluent Spanish, so I requested an assignment where I could exercise that skill. Nicaragua fit the bill perfectly. Imagine my surprise when I discovered that my textbook knowledge of Spanish had not prepared me to interact fluently with the people I met. Oh, I had practiced my skills in short study programs in Mexico and Ecuador. However, my new job required me not just to interact with college students and urban professionals, but also to form relationships with rural farming families whose vocabularies were filled with colorful local words and phrases, many of which were used only in Nicaragua. I learned the local words for the corner stores ubiquitous in rural communities, for seasonal foods, and for hair colors and textures and body types. I learned the names of Nicaragua's celebrities, political figures, and pop stars, as well as slang words and old sayings. I learned over a dozen words just for talking about corn: a word for the first tiny ears you could boil in a soup; a word for the special tortillas made from fresh, as opposed to dried, corn (a national favorite); another for the corn you could grill over a fire and eat from the cob; and yet another for the baked corn cookies made with farmer's cheese and served with sweet, strong coffee.

You see my point. You can memorize all the business terms in the world, but until you immerse yourself in the hustle and bustle of the business world, you cannot claim full fluency in the language. What does the word "disruption" mean to you? It means something very specific in business. The same with "pivot." And that's before you come to A/B testing, B2B, and B2C; funnels, personas, conversions, use cases, business models, and many other words you have heard and used many times but may mean something quite different to a business professional.

To increase your fluency in business lingo, watch a few minutes of Bloomberg Television each morning, or, as Michael did, pick the brains of colleagues and superiors at work. Incorporate business-focused media (websites, magazines, television programs, podcasts) into your reading, watching, and listening routines. To get started, choose three media outlets or publications to support your ongoing education. This could include newspapers such as the *Financial Times* or *Wall Street Journal*; magazines such as *Fortune, Forbes*, or *Business Insider*; or podcasts such as *Marketplace* from American Public Media or *How to Start a Startup* from the well-known business incubator Y Combinator. Whatever sources you use, make business language study a daily habit.

Finally, remember that industries and organizations build their own unique cultures, "the way we do things around here." When you use industry- and organization-specific vocabulary, you go a long way toward establishing yourself as an insider. That's important to keep in mind, particularly if you foresee a career change on your horizon. But you don't need to have worked at McKinsey to be able to use the vocabulary of management consulting. You simply need to find ways to expose yourself to the words and phrases in common usage in the industry, or all the different ways the companies on your short list refer to "corn."

This Adviser's Challenge will help ensure that you surround yourself with the language and culture of business.

Figure 3-6

> ▶ ADVISER'S CHALLENGE ◀
>
> ## ACHIEVE FLUENCY IN THE LANGUAGE OF BUSINESS
>
> ....
>
> ❏ **Set up an on-the-job language lab.** Make a conscious attempt to find out more about the language used by managers and leaders in their daily work.
>
> ❏ **Subscribe to one or two business publications.** Include print or digital versions of such publications as *Fortune* or *The Wall Street Journal*.
>
> ....
>
> ❏ **Look for YouTube videos and other audio or video business media.** Enter a term like "leadership" into the YouTube search bar and you will come up with thousands of offerings.
>
> ....
>
> ❏ **Start a dictionary of business terminology.** Whenever you see or hear a word you cannot precisely define, look it up and write it down.
>
> ....
>
> ❏ **Install an app such as Pocket (http://getpocket.com) on your computer browser or mobile device.** Pocket and other apps allow you to save reading material and other digital media in a queue for reading/watching/listening at a later time.
>
> ....
>
> ❏ **Turn it into a game.** Instead of just sitting back and enjoying a television program or movie where business figures into the plot, listen for new words you can add to your dictionary.

Congratulations on selecting your core curriculum, setting up your first class schedule, and immersing yourself in business language and culture. Next, we will get to the heart of your business education—how to build your business skills.

POINTS TO REMEMBER

1. Browse the world of MOOCs to see that they duplicate all of the courses offered in traditional MBA programs.
2. Structure your business education atop a solid foundation of core business concepts.
3. Make sure you delve into the three major categories included in any business curriculum: Quantitative and Financial Analysis, Management and Leadership, and Big-Picture Thinking.
4. Set up your core curriculum with four to six subjects drawn from all three of the major categories.
5. Construct your first class schedule by visiting the major MOOC platforms or using a search engine like Class Central.
6. Increase your exposure to business concepts, vocabulary, and companies by adding magazines, news shows, online publications, podcasts, and other business-focused media to your daily routines.

4

Sharpen Your Skills

Assembling Your Business Toolkit

ANDY loved working in the botanical production lab at Bio-dyne. His job as senior scientist in charge of preparing seedlings for commercial farms had turned his lifelong passion for biology into a successful career. Every day brought exciting new challenges that kept his creative juices flowing. His bosses trusted and respected him, often asking for his input on business-related topics far afield from biology. Andy wished he could answer those questions as accurately as ones involving his professional expertise. Then he discovered the No-Pay MBA blog. Problem solved, he thought, I'll get just what I need from a few online courses. After taking several MOOCs that gave him a firm foundation in the language of business, he moved on to skill-based courses. The experience thrilled the scientist in Andy, especially when he delved into the subject of negotiation. While taking a course on *Successful Negotiation: Essential Strategies and Skills,* he learned that a strong negotiator acts a lot like a good scientist, examining a problem or situation from multiple perspectives and then running through mental scenarios before taking action.

As he watched the course's video lectures, Andy found himself thinking about MaxFarm, a chemical supplier whose negotiation tactics had earned the company a reputation within the industry. MaxFarm's monopoly on certain key compounds enabled it to play hardball. Several years ago, Andy's boss Marty, frustrated by MaxFarm's "take it or leave it" approach, had halted all discussions with the supplier. Andy wondered if the negotiation skills he had been studying might make it possible to reach an agreement with MaxFarm that would allow Biodyne to reopen the relationship. After all, having access to MaxFarm's chemical compounds would allow Biodyne to develop much-needed new products.

Before approaching Marty for a green light, Andy sketched out three perspectives on the situation: his own view as the scientist running the Biodyne lab, MaxFarm's position as the supplier of an essential ingredient, and his boss's point-of-view as the Biodyne executive who had cut ties with MaxFarm. Andy considered what each party stood to gain or lose. After examining the situation from all three perspectives, Andy thought he might have zeroed in on a potential "ZOPA," a zone of possible agreement, where all of the parties could walk away satisfied. In the morning, he took the argument to his boss.

"I've been thinking about what you said in our last staff meeting about expanding our market," Andy began. "And I have a couple of ideas." Andy had learned the importance of leading off the conversation in a way that respected Marty's interest.

Marty's expression instantly brightened. "Oh yeah? I'm all ears."

Andy continued on a positive note, emphasizing the value of being able to develop new products. Finally, Marty green-lighted the initiative, on the condition that Andy spearheaded the negotiations. After inviting MaxFarm back to the negotiating table, Andy managed, after few tough rounds of talks, to reestablish a relationship that ended up allowing Biodyne to launch several new product lines.

Once you have learned the language of business by studying the core curriculum, you'll want to roll up your sleeves and start building specific business skills. Like Andy, you may find that some subjects inspire you more than others. Some you can immediately put to work on the job; others you will store in your business skills toolbox for later use.

In this chapter, we will explore the skills that everyone studying business should acquire and develop, starting by defining the major categories of business skills: Quantitative and Financial Analysis, Management and Leadership, Big-Picture Thinking, Communication-Storytelling, and Technology. Then, we will explore five specific skills in depth:

- Financial Modeling (Quantitative and Financial Analysis)
- Negotiation (Management and Leadership)
- Project Management (Management and Leadership/ Technology)
- Business Process Analysis (Quantitative and Financial Analysis/Management and Leadership)
- New Product Development (Big-Picture Thinking)

Note: I have reserved exercises for communication and storytelling for Chapter 6, where you will learn how to craft your personal communication plan.

Think Skills, Not Seat Time

While you can rely on MOOCs for both your foundational and advanced business education, you should think beyond the virtual classroom. What will you do with your education? Or, to put it another way, what skills will you learn and how will you use them to forward your career? Just sitting in a classroom or clicking your way through an online course won't land you a job or win you a promotion or attract investors to your new business idea, unless you can put your education to work in the real world. An education is not the sum total of hours spent in the classroom or a gilt-edged degree hanging on your wall; it's a key to solving problems and performing tasks that employers and investors value. Money chases value, not *vice versa*.

The most progressive voices in higher education have been advocating for "competency-based education," meaning that degrees should go to students according to how they demonstrate mastery by applying what they've learned, not the number of hours they have spent racking up credits in the classroom. Ryan Craig, author of the book *College Disrupted: The Great Unbundling of Higher Education,* champions the competency-based model.[1] As he and colleague Daniel Pianko explained in *Inside Higher Ed,* "A bachelor's degree merely indicates that a student sat (or slept in a drunken stupor) through at least 120 credit hours of C-graded 'college-level' work."[2] A better model, they say, would allow employers to see concrete evidence of the work a student did to earn a degree. Many of those observers of the changes sweeping through higher education, including Craig, believe that MOOCs and other forms of online learning work best when they result in demonstrable mastery of a topic. Michelle Weise, senior research fellow in higher education at the Clayton Christensen Institute for Disruption, took the argument a step further when she explained in the *Harvard Business Review* that students should strive for "mastery of a subject regardless of the time it takes to get there." She concluded that "learning is fixed, and time is variable."[3]

In the world of MOOCs, time is your ally. Kristof, the banker you met in Chapter 1, found introductory finance and accounting courses a breeze. He skipped through many of the introductory modules of such courses so that he could plunge right into the more advanced techniques he needed to advance his career. Other students (myself included) may need to go more slowly, dusting off their high school math skills before even attempting a finance course. Your self-directed business education program allows you to take the time you need to learn essential skills, which may mean skipping over what you already know or taking an occasional detour into some prerequisite material.

Focusing on competencies rather than on completing a certain number of required courses will also help you weather the rapid changes in the world of MOOCs and online learning. Case in point: When MOOCs first appeared, they cost nothing, even for a certificate of completion. Then, Coursera and edX introduced "verified" certificates for a fee. That soon became the rule, rather than the exception. Most recently, Coursera has placed the graded elements of many of its courses (quizzes, tests, and assignments) behind pay walls. If you view your education as a laboratory for acquiring and testing skills, you will not necessarily need a verified certificate. For example, Vijay needed to know how to manage a virtual team for the tech company he had just set up. Halfway through his first course on project management, he had already picked up many of the skills he needed to manage his team more effectively. He may never need a certificate at all.

The only sure thing in life is change. The world of MOOCs will undergo changes even the experts cannot predict. But I will bet my uncle Dave's farm on this: Providers will make more and more university-level learning materials and professional-caliber training modules available to the public, not just through MOOCs, but also through recorded talks, iTunes U, and even universities' own websites. This supports the argument that you should think in terms of skills, not when, where, and how you obtain those skills.

Gain Some Broad-Based Business Skills

As we did with the language of business, we will start with three major categories of broad-based skills: Financial and Quantitative Analysis, Management and Leadership, and Big-Picture Thinking. To this business skills framework (see Figure 4-1), we will add two other universally useful skills: Communication-Storytelling and Technology.

Financial and Quantitative Analysis

Business professionals work with numbers every day. To join their ranks you must understand the key concepts and language of finance. You should feel comfortable reading and interpreting financial statements, building simple financial models, making investment recommendations, and including quantitative analysis when making decisions where "the numbers" will strongly influence an outcome.

Management and Leadership

Even if you only report to yourself, you will need the management and leadership skills that help build solid relationships with others. Craig Hickman's classic book *Mind of a Manager, Soul of*

Figure 4-1. **Business Skills Framework**

FINANCIAL AND QUANTITATIVE ANALYSIS	MANAGEMENT AND LEADERSHIP	BIG-PICTURE THINKING	COMMUNICATION-STORYTELLING	TECHNOLOGY (a partial list)
• Read and interpret financial statements • Create a cash flow projection or budgeting tool using spreadsheets • Analyze and present data from a dataset • Make recommendations and decisions based on financial or other quantitative data	• Organize and manage a team to produce a specific deliverable or meet a specific goal • Delegate and supervise the work of others • Add value to a team • Conduct a negotiation • Take and give feedback • Identify, develop, and foster the talent of others • Cast a vision and inspire people to work toward it • Manage and/or reform repeating processes	• Assess the potential of a new project, business, or product line • Determine product-market fit • Describe the business model, value proposition, and unique selling points of a product or service • Understand and develop customer segments and personae • Use management frameworks to organize information and communicate it to others • Analyze the strategic position of an organization	• Give a presentation • Prepare a written report • Create an effective, concise, and visually appealing slide deck • Make a case for a point-of-view • Use stories to engage, inspire, and motivate people	Learn to use: • Email • Shared calendars • Videoconferencing • Project management software • Spreadsheets, word processing, slide presentations • Web-based technologies • Emerging technologies

a Leader described the difference. Managers, he argued, use their heads to guide their interactions with people; leaders follow their hearts. Managers are craftsmen; leaders are artists.[4] The most successful businesspeople know when and how to make the logical case for getting results and then inspire people to achieve those results. In a corporate setting you must know how to organize a team to produce a deliverable; delegate, supervise, and evaluate the work of others; and contribute to a team's performance. In a startup situation, you must know how to manage relationships with investors, suppliers, customers, and other stakeholders.

Big-Picture Thinking

Success depends on such sweeping skills as creating a vision of the future, thinking strategically, harnessing innovation, and controlling "big picture" variables that can make or break a business. You must know how to analyze the strategic position of an organization, understand market opportunities, and assess the potential of a new product or service. Such high-level analysis often combines concepts from many disciplines, including leadership, finance, entrepreneurship, and marketing. However, even the biggest ideas will die stillborn if you cannot communicate them effectively to others.

Communication and Storytelling

To navigate successfully through many conversations that occur during a typical workday, you need to employ a broad array of communications skills. In addition to a strong grasp of business language, you must know how to write and speak clearly, concisely, and compellingly, not only with words, but also with a variety of communications media. And you must know how to listen just as carefully as you speak. Effective communicators tell great stories. As Ed Sabol, founder of NFL Films and winner of over forty Emmy awards famously put it, "Tell me a fact, and I'll learn. Tell me a truth, and I'll believe. But tell me a story, and it will live in my heart forever."[5]

Technology

While you do not need to become a computer programmer to succeed in business, you must know how use the latest organization, communication, and productivity technologies. These include email, shared calendars, videoconferencing, messaging (e.g., Slack), file sharing, project management software, and such standard software solutions as spreadsheets, word processing, and slide presentations. You must keep your eyes open for the next technology or risk losing an important competitive edge.

At this point you should take a long, hard look at your current level of business skills.

Figure 4-2

► ADVISER'S CHALLENGE ◄

RATE YOUR CURRENT BUSINESS SKILLS

Use the Business Skills Framework in Figure 4-1 to complete this exercise. For each bulleted skill, rate yourself on a scale from 1 to 5, where 1 is rank beginner and 5 is true expert. If you score a 1 on a subject, you need to start with a beginner's course. A score of 2 or 3 indicates that you might take more challenging courses focused on practical application, while a 4 means that you should ↓

try to apply your skill more fully on the job. Of course, if you score a 5, you can move onto a subject where you racked up a lower score.

....

❏ **1 = First Year MBA Student:** I'm not sure I even know the terminology used to describe this skill.

....

❏ **2 = Intern:** I understand the basic concept but have never actually performed this skill.

....

❏ **3 = Junior Analyst:** I have performed this skill a few times but do not yet feel perfectly comfortable with it.

....

❏ **4 = Manager:** I frequently use this skill but know I could develop it more fully.

....

❏ **5 = Executive:** I know how to use this skill and could even teach it to others.

This exercise should have helped sharpened your focus on which skills to emphasize in your self-directed MBA curriculum.

Set Up Your Learning Laboratories

Ellen began her career with a narrow focus, enrolling in a performing arts conservatory where she studied vocal performance. She would often spend up to six hours per day singing in classes, rehearsals, and independent practice. Every waking moment took her one step closer to becoming a professional musician and landing a role as a principal performer in an opera company. Music was her life.

When she moved to New York City after graduation, however, she found it a lot harder than she had imagined to secure one of those coveted spots with an opera company. Dozens of auditions did land her a couple of small parts for the summer opera season, but she ended up waitressing to make ends meet. Three years of that precarious existence pushed her no nearer to her dream. "I can't keep racing down this dead-end street," she decided. "I've got to make a change." Then, as so often happens in life, she got a lucky break, just not the one she imagined. A regional opera company offered her a behind-the-scenes job as a junior member of its management team. Why not take it, she thought; it might eventually lead to a performing role.

To her surprise, Ellen loved her new job and became quite good at it. It wasn't the uncreative drudgery she had imagined. No matter how talented the performers, the show could not go on without the management work that supported it. When her hard work made that happen, she felt as important as the lead singer in *La Bohème*. While Ellen continued to perform from time to time, she came to appreciate the security (and the reliable paycheck) that came with a management job. As she rose in the ranks, she soon found herself managing a small staff and a hefty budget. That role tested the limit of her management skills.

With a full-time job, Ellen could not go back to school to acquire the skills she needed. MOOCs offered the perfect solution. She took a few courses in business basics, then began tailoring her studies to important tasks at work. A course on financial management and decision making helped her handle her budgeting responsibilities. Then a course in human resources management taught her what she needed to know to recruit and manage a top-notch team. Course by course, she worked toward the completion of her MBA equivalent.

Remember the Mastery Pyramid in Chapter 3? Even the best business education does not amount to a pile of sand if you don't experiment with it in a real-life laboratory. Like Andy and Ellen, you may already be working in a learning lab. But what if your job doesn't provide any ready opportunities to test your business skills? What if you are unemployed or working in a job that does not lend itself to practicing what you're learning? Not to worry. You can look for a mentor in a department of your company where you do not currently work, or seek out volunteer positions, internships, self-directed role-playing exercises, or case studies, anywhere you can set up shop and put your new skills under the microscope as you apply them to real or virtual situations. While I was studying accounting and financial management, for example, I took a volunteer job as the treasurer of the employee association at work. It provided a small, safe opportunity for me to practice my new skills without the risk of making a fatal mistake.

Most students can benefit from multiple learning laboratories. The best ones offer opportunities to:

- Match work that needs to be done to the skills you are learning.
- Do actual work and solve real problems.
- Test your skills on your own schedule.
- Make mistakes and gain feedback in a safe environment.

Whatever labs you choose, they should, in the long run, help you acquire and sharpen the five most essential business skills.

Master Five Essential Business Skills

Having rated your current level of mastery in the major skill categories, you have identified your strengths and weaknesses and determined where, over time, you may need to take MOOCs to fill the gaps. If you scored all 5s on the Rate Your Current Business Skills test (Figure 4-2), you can comfortably skip the rest of this chapter. But like most of us, you could probably stand to sharpen any or all of these skills, no matter your current level of proficiency. The next Adviser's Challenge (Figure 4-3) will guide you to learn and practice five essential skills, drawn from across the major skill sets. You will almost surely need them if you pursue a lifelong career as a business professional:

1. Build a financial model (Quantitative and Financial Analysis).
2. Become a stronger negotiator (Management and Leadership).
3. Manage a project team using contemporary project management software (Management and Leadership/Technology).
4. Assess a repeating business process and recommend ways to improve efficiency (Quantitative and Financial Analysis/Management and Leadership).
5. Analyze product-market fit for an entrepreneurial venture (Big-Picture Thinking).

I suggest you quickly scan the whole challenge then select one component of it for your current needs. You need not plow through A-B-C-D-E in order. You may complete one section, pause, then tackle another as needed or when you feel motivated to dive into it and, of course, you can skip any that you cannot imagine using in a million years. Note: As mentioned previously, I have reserved exercises for communication and storytelling for Chapter 6, where you will learn how to craft your personal communication plan.

Figure 4-3

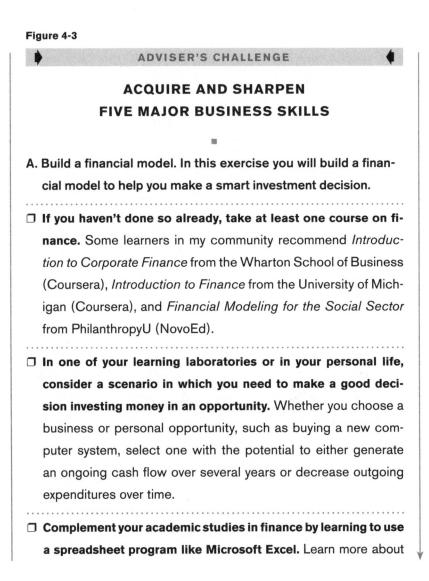

➤ ADVISER'S CHALLENGE ◀

ACQUIRE AND SHARPEN
FIVE MAJOR BUSINESS SKILLS

■

A. Build a financial model. In this exercise you will build a financial model to help you make a smart investment decision.

. . . .

❐ **If you haven't done so already, take at least one course on finance.** Some learners in my community recommend *Introduction to Corporate Finance* from the Wharton School of Business (Coursera), *Introduction to Finance* from the University of Michigan (Coursera), and *Financial Modeling for the Social Sector* from PhilanthropyU (NovoEd).

. . . .

❐ **In one of your learning laboratories or in your personal life, consider a scenario in which you need to make a good decision investing money in an opportunity.** Whether you choose a business or personal opportunity, such as buying a new computer system, select one with the potential to either generate an ongoing cash flow over several years or decrease outgoing expenditures over time.

. . . .

❐ **Complement your academic studies in finance by learning to use a spreadsheet program like Microsoft Excel.** Learn more about applying financial modeling and decision making in the real world in a more advance course, such as *Intro to Financial Modeling* on the Udemy platform, taught by finance professionals Symon He and Brandon Young.

☐ **Use what you have learned about finance to build a financial model** that compares various scenarios for the decision in question.

☐ **In a real or imagined situation, present your model to the decision maker,** highlighting your key conclusions and how you arrived at them.

B. **Become a stronger negotiator. Here you will develop your negotiation techniques to produce better outcomes in all kinds of scenarios.**

☐ **Take a MOOC on negotiation.** I strongly recommend *Successful Negotiation: Essential Skills and Strategies* (Coursera), one of the most popular MOOCs of all time.

☐ **Think about the various negotiations you conduct in your daily life.** You engage in so many every day, from discussing who will pick up dinner on the way home from work to asking your boss for a raise. Identify strategies you might use to achieve the desired outcome.

☐ **Select an upcoming negotiation at home or at work.** Prepare for the negotiation using the techniques you have learned. Write down your negotiation plan.

☐ **After the negotiation, reflect on what worked and what didn't.**

☐ **Record the elements of your personal negotiation** style in a document you can consult the next time you enter into a negotiation.

■

C. Manage a project team using contemporary project management software. Now you will lead a team to produce a high-quality, on-time result using one or more of the many online tools for team collaboration.

☐ **Study project management by taking a MOOC** such as *Fundamentals of Project Planning and Management* from the University of Virginia (Coursera).

☐ **Explore some of the free project management and collaboration tools you can access online, such as Trello and Asana.** If you do not currently use a cloud-based file sharing and storage program like Google Drive or Dropbox, start now. Take a look at some of the excellent YouTube videos on using these tools. If you need additional help getting started, Udemy provides more comprehensive courses on all of the most commonly used workplace productivity programs.

☐ **Take the lead on a project in one of your learning laboratories.** Ideally, the project should involve a multi-person team working over a period of weeks or months to achieve a measurable result. Again, you can pick a business project, such as training a sales team, or a personal undertaking, such as planning and pulling off a big wedding.

☐ **Use the techniques you studied in your project management course and your chosen collaboration software** to ensure that the project concludes on time and within budget.

☐ **Ask the other members of the team to provide candid feedback** on how you managed the project.

■

D. Assess a repeating business process and recommend ways to improve efficiency. In this assignment, you will apply operations management techniques to a repeating business process.

☐ **Study operations management by taking a MOOC** such as *Introduction to Operations Management* (Coursera), one of the foundational courses offered by the Wharton School of Business.

☐ **Make a list of repeating business processes in one or more of your learning laboratories.** You can look at most aspects of business and life as processes: stocking shelves, filing important records, and responding to customer inquiries; mowing the lawn, doing the laundry, or cleaning an apartment. Christian Terwiesch, the professor who teaches *Introduction to Operations Management,* cites examples of operational efficiency ranging from cooks making sandwiches to doctors seeing patients in a busy hospital.

☐ **Select one of the repeating processes for a thorough analysis.** Choose one that takes place over a relatively short time span and repeats frequently enough for you to observe multiple cycles of the process.

☐ **Use the techniques you studied in your operations management course** to analyze the repeating process.

☐ **Prepare a report or presentation** summarizing your findings and recommending changes that will improve efficiency.

■

E. Analyze product-market fit for an entrepreneurial venture. Finally, you will practice using customer development techniques drawn from the Lean Startup methodology.

☐ **If you haven't already taken a MOOC** on entrepreneurship, do so. I particularly like the excellent course *How to Build a Startup* (Udacity), taught by serial entrepreneur Steve Blank, a major contributor to the modern methods of entrepreneurship. The course offers a well-crafted introduction to the techniques of Lean Startup, along with plenty of encouragement for you to get out of the classroom and into contact with customers.

☐ **Identify an entrepreneurial project you plan or hope to launch.** You might even think about one you could suggest to your employer.

☐ **Use what you have learned about entrepreneurship to create an initial sketch of the product or service,** including a description of your target customers, their location, their main problems or "pain points," and to what extent your proposed product or service will better fulfill their customer experience. Try using a tool like the Business Model Canvas to record your assumptions.

☐ **Conduct interviews with seven to ten target customers.** In each interview, focus on the causes of the main "pain points" they suffer.

☐ **Use what you learn during the interviews to revise and update your initial business model sketch.** Take special note of any assumptions you should revise in light of the feedback you have gathered.

☐ **Summarize your findings in a plan** that you or an imagined entrepreneur might successfully execute.

After you have finished one or more of these exercises, retake the Rate Your Current Business Skills test (Figure 4-2). Can you see measurable improvement in your mastery of these important skills? Have you pinpointed other skills you want to acquire and develop? Use what you have learned to continue refining your own personal skill development curriculum.

Craft Your Own Skill-Based Challenges

Jerome understands very well the importance of putting new skills into practice immediately. As an instructional designer for a software company, he spends his days designing training modules that enable students to put what they are learning to work in hands-on practice exercises. Jerome didn't always consider himself an educator; he earned his bachelor's degree in computer science. Early on he fell in love with the idea of online learning and saw a terrific opportunity to advance his career and follow his passion by taking a job with a large tech firm in his city that needed computer scientists with an understanding of online learning techniques. From the first day on the job he knew he had found his true calling.

Of course, Jerome immediately felt drawn to the wonderful new world of MOOCs. By studying business online, he hoped to kill two birds with one stone: learn about state-of-the-art online education while acquiring a first-rate business education himself. It was a perfect match. The learning helped him design his own programs while putting what he was learning into practice. As he told me, "Sometimes you have to invent a reason to practice. I don't intend to become an accountant, but when I studied accounting, I *was* an accountant. My conversations at home, my family budget, my interests at work—everything was tinged with that worldview. You have to really immerse yourself as you're taking a class. But more than anything else, a practical task really solidifies the learning in my head."

POINTS TO REMEMBER

1. Think of your business education in terms of skills and competencies you want to master.
2. Take stock of your essential business skills, focusing on the three main categories of the business curriculum (Quantitative and Financial Analysis, Management and Leadership, and Big-Picture Thinking) and two crosscutting business skill sets (Communication-Storytelling, and Technology).
3. Select a learning laboratory (or laboratories) where you can practice your business skills as you acquire them.
4. Use the second Adviser's Challenge in this chapter to add skills to your repertoire.
5. Invent your own skill-based challenges to put your skills into practice in real settings.

5

Create Your Career

Charting a Professional Path

CORY liked to take the path less traveled. "When I was young, some successful people encouraged me to attend university, while others encouraged me to find myself before pursuing a formal education," he says. "Weighing my options, I decided not to pursue postsecondary education at that stage of my life; instead I began to develop my interpersonal and problem-solving skills." When his classmates went the expected route, enrolling in colleges and universities, Cory took a sales job in the local office of TeleNex, a multinational communications company known for its commitment to employee development. Thus began a lifelong experiment in personal career development.

One of his early mentors advised Cory to take stock of his strengths, talents, and interests and to build his future career based on that foundation. Taking that advice to heart, Cory reflected on the math classes that had so engrossed him in high school. "Most people hated word problems, but I always loved identifying patterns based on what sequence or shape comes next, or figuring out how many fences Alex and Julie could paint together in a day. I realized that I like considering a complex situation and figuring out the solution that fits." How, he wondered, could he turn that fascination into a career advantage? Perhaps he should move into marketing, where his skills might help TeleNex better target potential customers.

After a successful stint in the marketing department, Cory moved into client relations, where he became interested in process improvement. Eventually he took his growing arsenal of skills to some of the best-known businesses in the fields of technology and management consulting. Cory credits much of his success to the disciplined way he has developed and managed his strengths, a strategy that now includes taking a number of well-chosen MOOCs. "I knew I wasn't willing to go all the way back to square one and sit through the distribution requirements of a bachelor's degree. I needed something flexible and adaptable that would allow me to study just what I needed, when I needed it."

His MOOC-based business education led him into commercial banking, a profession that seemed ideally suited to his skills with pattern recognition, adaptability, and quick decision making. To his chagrin, however, the bank he had targeted as a perfect fit for him and his talents turned him down after a lengthy interview he thought he had aced. The interviewers had seemed genuinely intrigued by his nontraditional background. One of those interviewers later confided that the panel had passed over Cory in favor of an internal candidate and encouraged him to reapply in the future.

One year later, after successfully completing additional online courses in marketing, strategic thinking, and managerial accounting, he reapplied at the bank that had rejected him and ended up landing a job the company had not yet advertised. Cory now spends his days using quick thinking, problem solving, and strategy to manage a complex commercial loan portfolio.

Of all the skills you acquire on your quest to become a business professional, none will serve you better than the ability to develop and manage your own career. To create my own MBA-style business education (and ultimately to write this book), I thoroughly researched what happens behind the walls of the top traditional MBA programs. In the end, I was amazed by how much time, effort, and resources business schools spend to help students better match their education to the world of work. Whether in discussions with mentors and advisers or through an intensive coaching program, students conduct rigorous self-assessments, reflect on their past accomplishments, research business careers, and develop detailed lists of potential employers, all geared to helping them find the right career fit after graduation. While you may at some point want to enlist the services of a professional career coach or counselor, you will never find one who knows you better than the one who lives inside your own head. Develop that coach's skills, and your career will flourish.

Coach Yourself

Whether you are just starting out your own great career experiment, orchestrating a career shift, hoping to rise through the ranks at your current workplace, or planning to launch a new enterprise from scratch, you should think of your education as a laboratory where you can experiment with ways you can achieve the success you seek. Traditional programs structure that lab experience for you. In a self-directed program, you must learn to think strategically about your business education and conduct experiments that will help you discover your true calling. At this middle stage of your education, having gained some exposure to the business curriculum and some specific business skills, you should begin to think seriously about your short- and long-term career goals. "Where do I want to go? How will I get there?"

Imagine that you are taking a second-semester business school course designed to prepare you for a summer internship and the more practical, hands-on work that comprises the latter half of the program. Many business schools offer such courses on self-knowledge, self-understanding, and career management. Students usually love these courses, many of which you can obtain in book form. As you begin your career self-coaching program, consider hiring such a "coach in a book." One of the best is *Springboard: Launching Your Personal Search for Success*, based on a popular course taught by Professor G. Richard Shell at the Wharton School of Business. *Springboard* will help you direct your strengths and passions toward a deeply satisfying and richly rewarding career. Or you might consult *The Art of Self-Coaching*, by executive coach Ed Batista, which is drawn from his course of the same title offered at Stanford's Graduate School of Business. Like any good career coach, these business professors insist that you begin with a clear-eyed self-assessment.

Assess Yourself

At a workshop with some of the business students in my network, we started the day's activities by taking one of the many character and personality assessments available online. As people finished a short quiz, the videoconference line bubbled with excited chatter.

"What was your top characteristic? Mine was Love of Learning."

"Interesting! I had that as number five. My number one was Curiosity."

"I had Analytical Thinking. Did anyone else have that?"

"Of course you did. You're an engineer! That was like number twenty for me. I had Empathy, Creativity, and Problem Solving right at the top. But that makes sense, too, because I've gotten really into customer development, which is all about those traits."

This kind of excitement often erupts when you begin to study one of the most fascinating topics in any business curriculum: yourself. Even if you have always reflected on who you are and where you are going in life, you may not have looked at yourself through the lens of business. When you do, you may make some interesting discoveries.

Many business schools offer or even require detailed personal assessments, in which students answer a great number of multiple-choice questions about themselves, their habits, and their preferences. The results indicate what sort of work environments you might enjoy, how you might react in certain business situations, and which specific careers you should consider. While such assessments do not guarantee a successful career, they do get you thinking about "life after education." Cory's mentor pointed him to *StrengthsFinder 2.0*, a career management book that includes a personal strengths inventory. There, he received some strong reinforcement for his career hunches about problem solving, quick thinking, and adaptability.

The Adviser's Challenge in Figure 5-1 will help you take stock of your personal preferences and tendencies and what they may tell you about plotting your professional career path.

Figure 5-1

> ► **ADVISER'S CHALLENGE** ◄
>
> ## CONDUCT A DETAILED SELF-ASSESSMENT
>
> ☐ **Select and complete two quiz-based self-assessments.** Take one personality-based assessment, such as the Myers-Briggs Type Indicator, and one career-focused assessment, such as Career Leader or MAPP. Personality assessments tend to paint a general picture of how you interact with others and how you approach problems. Career-focused assessments zero in on the business careers that may appeal to you.
>
> **Note that many of the higher-quality assessments charge a fee for complete results.** Some will let you access a shortened, free version or take the complete quiz at no charge, but with only a limited set of results. Consider some of these examples:
>
> - Myers-Briggs Type Indicator
> - VIA Character Survey
> - California Psychological Inventory
> - Sokanu
> - Career Leader
> - MAPP
>
> ☐ **Reflect on your past work and education experiences, asking yourself the following questions:**
>
> - What work experiences have I enjoyed the most?
> - Why did I like that work?
> - What sort of work do I dream of doing?
> - Why does that work appeal to me?
> - Would I derive both satisfaction and a decent income from that work?

- Can I imagine myself doing that work five or ten years from now?
- Which business subjects do I love?
- Why do I love those subjects?
- Does my business education match my vision of a successful career?

· ·

❏ **Look for common threads or themes.** You should look for certain patterns that recur in your life. Make a two-column list; label one column "Recurring Themes" and the other "Types of Work." For example, you may feel most comfortable "working alone in a quiet space," or you might prefer doing your job in a "social environment" with a roomful of coworkers chatting on the phone and typing madly on their keyboards. The former preference might lead you to consider such job titles as "business analyst," while the latter might point you toward "sales and marketing" or "fast-paced startup," where you would work in a cubicle or open work environment that offers a lot of social interaction.

It's hard to cast a cold, clear eye on our innermost selves. Try to adhere to the principles of nonjudgment and appreciative inquiry. A nonjudgmental approach seeks an accurate picture of reality uncolored by value judgments, such as "I could make a ton of money in investment banking." In reality, you may love writing and communication more than high-level finance, which argues for a position in the business media rather than one at Behemoth Bank. Your education should prepare you to pursue your true calling, not necessarily the heftiest salary or the most prestigious title. Appreciative inquiry means looking for strengths rather than weaknesses. Some experts on power and leadership believe that success depends on shoring up your weaknesses; others insist that it comes from playing to your strengths. In this case, you should focus on the latter school of thought: "What are my most positive attributes? How can I best take advantage of those traits? What sort of work will let me show off my strengths?"

Patricia, trained in fine arts, took a personal inventory after spending several years working in the fashion industry in New York but had ended up feeling disappointed in her stalled career trajectory. "I thought I wanted to be an artist, but after some deep thinking about myself, I decided that while I really wanted to do something creative with my life, I was better at storytelling than painting. That eventually led me to my dream job as a developmental editor, helping authors become better storytellers. It's funny. My strength is helping people overcome a weakness." Patricia gained the skills she needed by interning with a literary agent, who later became her partner. Now she plans to enroll in *Small Business Management* (Saylor.org), a MOOC that will add business acumen to her repertoire of skills.

Your process of self-discovery, coupled with your exposure to new business ideas, can yield some unexpected results. Roland, a human resources manager, grew fascinated with design thinking, entrepreneurship, and product development. Before starting his MOOC-based business studies, he would never have predicted that these subjects would strike his fancy. He had felt far more attracted to operations management, business process improvement, and leadership. But his self-assessment confirmed his aptitude for out-of-the-box thinking, and his Meyer-Briggs personality test revealed him as a creative, empathetic, and sensitive individual. His business career inventory suggested that he would find a good match in any job involving a high degree of personal interaction and problem solving, possibly in marketing, new product development, or entrepreneurship. On the other hand, Roland knew himself well enough to know that any position must also offer the stability and predictability he craved. He wasn't at all interested in ditching his secure job to join a Silicon Valley startup, nor was he the type to spend his evenings tinkering in the garage or taking a second mortgage to finance a startup business. When the workday was done, he just wanted to relax at home over a nice meal and a glass of wine.

His introspection did, however, lead him to shift his thinking about his career. Of all his work experiences, he had felt most passionate about the time he had spent revamping the onboarding process for new hires in order to make their first days in the office more fun and interactive. "What if I went to my boss with a detailed plan to create a customer-oriented hiring process?" he thought. This project would tap into his predilection for entrepreneurship and design thinking without risking the safety of working in a big company. While the assessment he completed may have pegged him as an entrepreneur, it took Roland's own insight to recognize "intrapreneurship" as the ideal fit. Through the combination of business classes, self-assessment, and reflection, Roland has found great satisfaction at work.

Develop Your Hypotheses

When Eric Reis wrote *The Lean Startup*, he launched a cataclysmic shift in thinking about entrepreneurship. Rather than emphasize detailed and rigid business plans, Reis championed an experimental approach to launching a new enterprise. Like a good scientist, an entrepreneur should develop hypotheses (in this case, ideas about which new products customers will buy) that can be tested on a small scale before making a big investment. Implementing a detailed business plan can cost a small (or not-so-small) fortune, compared to testing a Minimum Viable Product with a targeted group of customers.[1] The latter affords entrepreneurs a relatively inexpensive way to learn what works and doesn't work with the target market.

This same philosophy underpins the concept of Design Thinking, a topic you may want to add to your self-guided curriculum. As Professor Jeanne Liedtka of the University of Virginia explains in the popular MOOC on the subject, *Design Thinking for Innovation*, the smart designer never goes "all-in" with a single big idea but rather places many small bets with far less risk.[2] Instead of retooling the whole factory to build a new bicycle without knowing whether customers will fall in love with it, you can build a prototype that customers can test-drive and evaluate. With user input, you can decide whether to implement or adjust your plans.

As you craft your education and your career path, you can think of yourself as both an entrepreneur and a designer. You may not have embarked on your MOOC-based business education with the principles of Lean Startup and Design Thinking in mind, but your education already embodies important elements of both concepts. Instead of taking out a gigantic loan, quitting your job, and investing two years to advance your career with a big expensive degree, you have placed a small bet on an educational path that will allow you to shift course as you gather new information. Going forward you can use both approaches to tailor your education and shape your career trajectory. Even if your career plan starts as a hunch, as it did for both Cory and me, you can greatly benefit from testing a hunch. Write it down, mull it over, test-drive it, adjust it, and try it again.

Your experimentation with various hypotheses will help you discover what I call Career-Self Fit, the ideal convergence of your unique talents, work style, and life goals with a job and a career. To generate useful hypotheses, you must assemble all available evidence, just the way a scientist does. For career purposes, the evidence includes past work experiences, insights obtained from business courses, and a careful self-assessment. With your own evidence in hand, try filling out the Industry/Company/Role Finder. To show you how to do it, I've added notes drawn from my own evidence in Figure 5-2.

Figure 5-2. **Industry/Company/Role Finder**

INDUSTRY	COMPANY	ROLE
1. International Development	1. U.S. Agency for International Development 2. My own consulting company	1. Program management 2. Entrepreneur/principal/manager
2. Education	1. College or University 2. My own consulting company	1. Teacher 2. Entrepreneur/teacher/principal/manager
3. Educational Technology	1. An ed-tech startup 2. My own consulting company	1. Product developer/project manager 2. Entrepreneur

As you know from reading the introduction to this book, I have always loved to travel, learn new languages, and immerse myself in foreign cultures. That naturally led me to the world of international development. You also know about my passion for online education, which made me think about working in the field of education, more specifically the MOOCs, where education and technology intersect. My own online business education convinced me that I would find the greatest fulfillment in an entrepreneurial and/or managerial role. Initially, my Industry/Company/Role Finder contained three hypotheses; yours might range from two to six. Settling for only one indicates too much inflexibility with respect to possible career options. More than six suggests you should more narrowly focus your thought experiments.

In his 2005 commencement address at Stanford University, Steve Jobs described building a career as "connecting the dots."[3] What dots have you already connected? What dots do you see in your future? Think creatively about your dots, looking for some unconventional, possibly surprising ones. Jobs went on to explain how an early interest in calligraphy translated into an appreciation for beautiful fonts that became important later in his career, especially when designing the first Macintosh computer. The New York University Robert F. Wagner School of Public Service recommends a similar visioning process it calls the Tracks Exercise. This exercise advises students to think of their future careers in terms of a set of jobs that appeal to them and the career "tracks" (courses, assignments, internships, and jobs experiences) that can help them arrive in one of those positions.[4]

Let your mind soar. Remain playful, imaginative, freewheeling as you consider your future prospects. Remember, you are not committing to any one industry/company/role; you're just test-driving ideas that might land you in the best possible Career-Self Fit. Even if you currently work in an industry you love and for a company that treats you well, you may want to make a major career shift at some point in your life. You should keep formulating and testing hypotheses throughout your life, even if you keep coming back

to the same Career-Self Fit. Throughout this book I have emphasized three results you might get from your self-administered MBA
equivalent: a) landing a dream job, b) climbing the ladder at your
current employer, and c) starting your own business. Who knows,
you may go from A to B to C or even from C back to A. Testing
hypotheses will help you make those transitions.

Test Your Hypotheses

Take a moment to review the Mastery Pyramid from Chapter 3.
Your progression through the various levels of the pyramid
should bring you ever closer to your Career-Self Fit. At the first
two levels you explore the full business landscape, taking it all in,
absorbing information from a variety of business disciplines, and
getting a feel for what practitioners of those disciplines actually
do at work. At this point you are not committing to a particular
industry/company/role. You are just gathering the information you
will need to make the transition from general business skills at the
second level to the specific, industry-related skills at the third level.

Gradually, you will sign up for courses that resonate with your
growing interest in a particular discipline. Once you reach that
third level, you should test your various hypotheses with every
MOOC you take. If Introduction to Marketing turned you on, you
will most likely enroll in Advanced Marketing, Digital Marketing,
and Brand Management. The material will become increasingly
valuable to you as you progress toward implementing your new
knowledge and skills. You can further test your assumptions
about a certain industry/company/role with research, reading,
internships, short-term consultancies, informational interviews,

company visits, and business networking. During this final phase you are refining, improving, and, in some cases, rejecting one or more of your hypotheses. You may still be filling in a few gaps in your knowledge and skill set, but you are drawing closer to at least a preliminary career commitment, be that advancement at your current employer, a new job, or an entrepreneurial adventure.

Figure 5-3. The Mastery Pyramid and Your Career

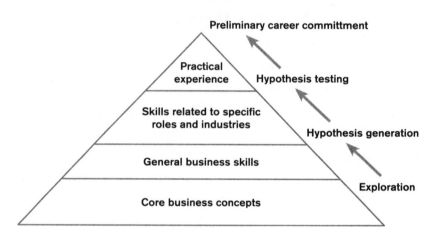

The next two chapters, on building your business network and applying your skills in the real world, will afford you an opportunity to test your hypotheses even further. Prepare yourself for some obstacles and surprises along the way. While freelancing market research for a pharmaceutical company, you might discover that full-time employment there will require intensive training in data analysis, a prospect that may either excite you or lead you to consider other options. Or an internship with a business law professor at a traditional business school might make you think twice about pursuing a career in that field because it ends up boring you to tears.

However you choose to test your hypotheses, you want to do it both from a worm's-eye view (boots on the ground, doing real work in a real job in the real world) and from a satellite's-eye view (above the fray, peering down at the whole landscape of options). Before you make a long-term commitment to a certain industry/company/role, you should test it in the short term and *vice versa*. Success in life and work almost always involves seeing both the little and the big picture. Little picture: "Do I really enjoy the work I'm doing, or am I fooling myself into thinking it will somehow become more thrilling down the line?" Big picture: "Does the work I love offer opportunities for growth, or will disruptive technology make it obsolete in five years?"

Take a Worm's-Eye View

When you test your hypotheses from a worm's-eye view, you gather information from the real world. What does it actually feel like when you do the work you have targeted as a good career option? While coursework can yield important insights, especially when it involves case studies and real-world examples, spending time in a real workplace and talking to people who work or have worked in the industries/companies/roles on your list will give you a better idea about what really goes on day in and day out. What does the work look like when you finally put your boots on the ground?

Of all the methods you might choose, internships and volunteer work yield the greatest results. The more closely the internship or volunteer project resembles the exact industry/company/role you are researching, the more you will learn from the experience. For example, if you are curious about a role as a management consultant, any experience in that world will tell you a lot. Perhaps you can offer your services *pro bono* to a small startup, a local nonprofit, or your uncle's coffee shop. If you have set your sights on management consulting with one of the Big Three (McKinsey, Bain & Company, The Boston Consulting Group), an internship at one of those firms will give you the boots-on-the-ground experience you need in order to understand what it would feel like working there full-time. (If nothing is available at one of the Big Three, an internship at a second-tier firm can provide similar experience.) No matter what sort of work you imagine doing, actually doing it can be a very different kettle of fish.

Jerome, the instructional designer you met in Chapter 4, knows exactly how to take the worm's-eye view. Not only does he fully immerse himself in his coursework and find ways to practice what he's learning, he also takes his new skills outside the classroom. While Jerome loves the work he does for the software company where he currently works, he has been testing the idea that he might really like to get into educational administration. To better understand what a management role at an education company might feel like, he recently began volunteering at an online education startup. Drawing on what he learned in *Financial Modeling for the Social Sector*, he eagerly got involved in a project where he could develop a financial model for forecasting operating expenses and setting prices on products. Not only did his work contribute to the goals of the organization, it also added to his boots-on-the-ground research into his ideal Career-Self Fit. By sitting in on the management meetings where people discussed and debated the organization's finances, Jerome realized that he much preferred designing software to debating pricing strategy. On the other hand, he has loved strategizing about company culture and staff development. These insights have helped Jerome refine his thinking about what his next career step will be.

Take a Satellite's-Eye View

Just as getting into the trenches and gathering real-world experience can help shape your future career, so can stepping back and contemplating your preferred industry/company/role from a more general perspective. Try to look five years, ten years, or even further into the future, imagining your work future at various points along the way. Again, think in terms of industry/company/role:

1. **Industry.** Where will this industry be in five, ten, and twenty-five years? In 2015, McKinsey & Company predicted that the industries poised for greatest long-term growth were automotive, agriculture, food processing, retail, and healthcare.[5] *Business Insider* identified general and operations managers, software applications development, computer system analysts, accountants and auditors, management analysts, computer and information systems managers, first-line supervisors of office and administrative workers, and personal financial consultants among the top-ten "best jobs of the future."[6] Don't pick a career based solely on its projected future, but do take into account that such fields as healthcare, management, and technology offer tremendous career opportunities.

2. **Company.** Is your current company (or the one you aspire to join) well managed, profitable, poised for growth? Do you see it

prospering far into the future? If you are striving for advancement with your current employer, study the company from an investor's point of view. Would you put your own money into the operation, hoping for a return on your investment? If you are planning to start your own company, do you see yourself running the business in the long term, or do you envision selling it within a few years so that you can move on to the next entrepreneurial adventure?

3. **Role.** What progress could you make over the years starting from your current position? What position above the next one would you like to win? Do you get excited about the work done by senior people in your industry or company? What would you like to be doing at the peak of your career?

Louisa, the musician you met in Chapter 3, offers an instructive example of taking both a worm's-eye and a satellite's-eye view of her career. Trained as a classical musician, she might have followed the well-traveled path to the concert stage, but she ended up in an entirely different world, working in product and customer strategy at a tech startup. It happened because she thought long and hard about her long-term future. Yes, she had always yearned to perform before appreciative audiences, but she knew the odds of that still happening fifteen years from now were slim to none. She was a gifted musical performer, but also had a knack for listening, an innate curiosity, and an abiding interest in entrepreneurship. Deciding to shift course away from musicianship, she saw marketing as a possible Career Self-Fit. Would marketing give her a chance to apply her nonmusical talents? To answer that question, she began flexing her marketing muscles in the field of classical music. Having cofounded a nonprofit arts organization while studying clarinet in graduate school, she had actually done a good deal of marketing and public relations in her quest to grow the organization. During that time, she had also landed a seasonal gig doing marketing and PR for the Cincinnati Opera. These experiences led her to a position with a marketing agency, where she worked as a consultant to a large and well-known consumer-goods firm.

With these experiences under her belt, Louisa contemplated her next move. Marketing seemed like a pretty good fit, but spending her entire career working for a huge corporation did not appeal to her at all. She wanted an environment more like a jazz quintet than a symphony orchestra. What about a small firm, or even a startup, especially one that somehow involved music? She wasn't even sure if such a company existed, but some careful research led her to LISNR, a startup that had developed a data transmission technology using sound waves. It wasn't exactly music, but it was close enough to pique her interest.

During the interview for a job as an account manager at LISNR, Louisa drew on her ability to visualize how sound travels, a skill she had honed at conservatory but never expected to use in a business setting. The interview panel loved her deep knowledge of acoustics and sound technology. Given her stint in marketing, they quickly agreed that she was by far the best candidate for the position. The moral of the story? Louisa imagined her life far into the future, but she didn't just dream about her future, she put her boots on the ground, testing her developing hypotheses with real work experiences. Has she found her life's true calling? Maybe, maybe not. Her continuing MOOC education may take her down many more surprising paths.

POINTS TO REMEMBER

1. Make career planning and management an integral part of your on-going business studies.
2. Begin your career planning by reflecting on your developing interests and accomplishments and conducting a detailed self-assessment.
3. Combine the results of your self-assessment with what you have learned from your business studies to generate hypotheses about the best industry/company/role for you.
4. Test and refine your hypotheses from a worm's-eye view.
5. Take a satellite's-eye view of your future.

6

Meet Your People

Building a Business Network

MOST business school grads build valuable networks during their studies. So can you. Arjan, a self-directed learner who moved to Düsseldorf, Germany, to follow his wife's career, offers an instructive example. Having long dreamed of starting his own tech company, he registered for *Beyond Silicon Valley: Growing Entrepreneurship in Transitioning Economies*. In that MOOC he learned how Cleveland, Ohio, a classic rust belt city, made a concerted push to boost the city's startup economy.

The MOOC's creator, Professor Michael Goldberg, urges his students to connect with like-minded people locally. Arjan went a step further, inviting people from his extended network to join the MOOC, as well as participate in a study group for sharing ideas and giving each other encouragement. The group attracted several local institutional partners, including a university, two local coworking spaces, and a nongovernmental organization that supported local entrepreneurship. At one meeting, entrepreneurs pitched their ideas to people who could actually help them make their dreams a reality, something that would seldom happen in a traditional walled-off classroom. As for the group's leader, Arjan ended up on the board of a local nonprofit organization focused on promoting networking for startup companies, where he has become an integral player in Düsseldorf's small but growing startup support system.

Networking involves much more than collecting business cards at meetings. It represents a well-thought-out strategy for creating connections who can help you succeed in your career. When it comes to networking, it's all about the *quality* of the connection, not the number of contacts in your email or social media accounts or even the prestigious title of the person who accepted your LinkedIn request. The contact must not only recognize your name but also happily act on your request for help.

Connect Strategically

Brandi studied business and journalism in college, and although she chose not to pursue a traditional MBA, she felt a few carefully selected MOOCs would round out her business education. She also obtained a bonus benefit: meeting and getting to know like-minded students. "I always look for what we have in common, and I love getting to meet people from different countries and different backgrounds." Brandi has made many new connections through her coursework on strategy, entrepreneurship, and marketing. "Being in the same classes together gives you a shared experience and a natural entry point. That way, getting to know someone new doesn't feel like an awkward first date," she says. Now that she feels comfortable making connections, she can strengthen her network and rely on those connections to further her career in marketing.

Even someone with a traditional MBA can strengthen his or her network. While Becky, a graduate of the Wharton School, initially took advantage of the network she built in school, landing a job as director of operations at a fast-growing startup that sells ethically sourced fashions, Becky keeps adding new connections, especially people who share her passion for working in startup companies. "Having some sort of common ground is essential," she says. "Now, the people I connect with the most are people who are also running startups, regardless of where they got their education. Knowing people who are actually doing what I'm doing is more important than whether we went to the same school."

You should build your network with specific objectives in mind. Through conversations with business school graduates, professors, and some highly successful people, I have found that the traditional business school network consists of what Robert Putnam, author of *Bowling Alone*, calls Bonds and Bridges.[1] I have applied some of his ideas about building social capital to the MOOC experience. In the world of online education, bonds refer to the deep connections that form among students based on their shared experience in school, while bridges represent connections with people in the business world. In Arjan's case, he began by bonding with the other students he invited into his *Beyond Silicon Valley* study group; then he built bridges to aspiring entrepreneurs and institutions in the local business community.

The bonds you form and the bridges you build will help you create and sustain your personal brand. If you graduate from Dartmouth's Tuck School of Business, you automatically share a brand identity with fellow students and alumni. Before you interview for jobs on Wall Street, you can contact Dartmouth alums that work there. Even if you make a cold call on a potential Wall Street employer, interviewers will have some understanding of the Dartmouth brand. Later, in Chapter 8, we will explore personal branding in greater depth, but for now, just keep in mind that you will need to present your unconventional business education in a way that will impress potential employers or investors. Your network can help you do that.

Your unique set of strategic connections set you apart from everyone else. Your network helps define and identify you as a serious, professional businessperson. With a lot of strategic thinking and a bit of ingenuity, you can build a star-studded network that rivals those created by students at Dartmouth, Harvard, or Stanford. You just need to focus on establishing relationships with people who can supply the information, access, or additional connections that can help you reach your career goals.

Make a Great First Impression

You probably know the old saying, "You never get a second chance to make a first impression." Business students in traditional programs take this adage to heart and work hard to cultivate a professional appearance and demeanor. Many students even wear suits to class. While I'm not suggesting that you replace your pajamas and fuzzy slippers with a business suit while taking online courses, I am recommending that you invest considerable time and thought into developing an online persona that will impress people with your professionalism. Imagine you have enrolled in a MOOC on Design Thinking. When you ask a pertinent question in the course's discussion forum, several students respond. One of them is HR Hank, who works as a recruiter in a human resources department at a big company. A natural networker, he accesses your LinkedIn profile, which includes a highly professional resume. He's impressed and asks to add you as a contact.

One great first impression can lead to another and another and another useful connection. Perhaps you know the concept "six degrees of separation." It proposes that any person stands no more than six handshakes away from anyone in the world. My friend Michael describes how it works. "Suppose I want to meet Pope Francis. I contact my friend Sarah, who is studying business at Georgetown University. She introduces me to her adviser, Father Bill Byron, the former president of Catholic University, who now teaches business ethics at Georgetown. Father Byron puts me in touch with Cardinal Dolan of New York, who, in turn, introduces me via email to the Pope. Voilà! I've accomplished my goal in four easy steps." If Michael were developing a brand where connections to the world of Catholicism would advance his career, he would have thought and acted strategically to develop that brand. And with each handshake, he would have made a great first impression as a serious and likable person with keen professional interests.

In my own case, early on in my studies, I spoke with a reporter who was researching the MOOC phenomenon. Over a year later, I asked her if she could effect an introduction to Steve Blank, the legendary entrepreneur whom she had interviewed for a different article. She gave me the name of Steve Blank's assistant, who eventually made it possible for me to invite him to interact for thirty minutes with some of the learners in my network. He agreed. It all started with a strong first impression, followed by two more. More than a year passed from first contact to a career-enhancing connection. Patience and persistence are also factors in building a successful business network.

As an online, independent student, you will form many of your most valuable connections via the Internet. While you certainly should plug into (or even help to build) face-to-face networks the way Arjan did, you, like all business professionals, will spend a lot of networking time in the digital world. In a 2013 survey, over 98 percent of employers reported using some form of social media for recruiting.[2] In the flesh-and-blood world you take care to make a good first impression with your appearance, your clothes, your warm smile, your firm handshake, and the ease with which you make eye contact. In the digital world, you must pay careful attention to the first impression you make with the content, clarity, tone, and sincerity of your messages.

A great first digital impression depends on the three main components of your personal brand: name, image, and story. Take the Adviser's Challenge in Figure 6-1.

Figure 6-1

▶   ADVISER'S CHALLENGE   ◀

PUT YOUR BEST FOOT FORWARD

❏ **List the digital media and platforms where people will meet you for the first time.** This will include the MOOC platforms where you take courses, all social media platforms, your personal website, and even your email account. You will want to craft the best first impression on each of these platforms.

❏ **Use your professional name.** You want to present a unified brand identity in all of your digital communications. Even in cases where you need an identifying "handle," select a name that comes close your professional name (i.e., LPickard1 rather than Sillycat2016).

❏ **Invest in press-release quality photos.** It pays to maintain a professional image. A photo taken by a professional will enhance your professional image much more effectively than a selfie. ▾

Adhere to the official or unofficial dress codes of your target audience. Blue jeans will suffice for viewers at Google but not for HR professionals at Goldman Sachs.

....

☐ **Tell your story.** All of your online profiles should tell a short story about who you are and where you want to go. Imagine someone asking you to tell him or her a little something about yourself. Do not limit your answer to your name, rank, and serial number, but do not launch into a novel-length tale of everything that's happened to you since you were born. Keep it to three or four well-crafted sentences. Adhere to the three Cs: clear, concise, compelling. Try to write something interesting: "I studied premed in college because I thought I wanted to be a doctor, but after spending two summers working as an orderly in an emergency room, I decided I wanted to get into the business side of the healthcare field. That's why I have been taking so many MOOCs from the top business schools. I absolutely love finance and economics."

When it comes to telling your story, you may need a small anthology of vignettes, each designed to appeal to different target readers. For instance, you might post a relatively formal and polished profile on LinkedIn, emphasizing your professional goals and accomplishments, while the narrative you use for your profiles on MOOC platforms might focus more on your past, present, and future educational experiences. For example, I used this narrative for my profiles on all the MOOC platforms where I took courses during my business education:

I'm an international development professional working on entrepreneurship and public-private partnerships in Kigali, Rwanda. I'm taking business courses as part of a project to construct a free MBA equivalent out of MOOCs. I'd love to connect with others who share my interests in development and entrepreneurship or my enthusiasm for MOOCs.

You can use your stories in other venues where you want to make a great first impression: telephone calls to potential connections, introductions in face-to-face encounters, and personal email messages. If you do it well, people will want to connect with you and find out more about you and your career goals.

Find (or Create) a Learning Community

It's evening in Ghent, Belgium. Kristof has returned home from work. After feeding his daughters and sending them to bed, he prepares to spend a couple of hours immersed in his current marketing MOOC. As he settles onto the couch with his laptop he hears the distinct chirp of a team notification from his Slack app. It's a message from Hillary. "Hey, have time for a quick video chat?" she asks.

"Sure thing," Kristof types back. He dons his headphones, and within a few seconds, he's looking at Hillary, just starting her day in sunny California. Her eighteen-month-old daughter squirms in her lap. Kristof and Hillary have been working as colleagues on a class project and have found it helpful to connect at this time of night/morning. Despite differences in gender, nationality, native language, and profession, the two of them have found that they share quite a few personal traits and values, including a knack for building relationships, even at a distance. Best of all, they've each found the perfect partner for studying and collaborating. When the two of them start kicking around ideas, they always come up with creative ideas neither of them would devise on their own. It's a classic case of 1 + 1 = 3.

Researchers have found that studying with others can reduce attrition, inoculate against burnout, and counter feelings of isolation and loneliness.[3] It can also help you more fully absorb course material. And let's be honest—doesn't studying with like-minded colleagues sound like more fun than studying solo by the light of your computer screen? But best of all, you are forming those vital first degrees of separation that can help you make the other connections you need to get the most out of your business education. You never know when one of those colleagues from your student days will prove critical to helping you make the all-important connection that helps you close a big sale, gain an interview with a prospective employer, or get into the same room with a likely investor in your new company.

In 2016, the *Huffington Post* ran a fascinating article titled "How 1 Tweet Led to an Internship in Silicon Valley."[4] The author, Mimi Zheng, had just graduated from school and could not decide whether to travel for a while or look for a job. As luck would have it, she had been following a blog by Smit Patel, a high school senior who had used social media to land an internship at Y Combinator in Silicon Valley. She sent him a tweet. Soon they were exchanging emails. Smit introduced Mimi to Mike, CEO of a company called Scriptrocks, who looked over Mimi's writing samples and awarded her an internship. It was like a pilot episode for "Social Media Meets Six Degrees of Separation."

You can meet new colleagues everywhere you go in the world of MOOCs. Most MOOCs include discussion forums. Unfortunately, as many MOOCs shift from scheduled courses to an on-demand or self-paced model, many discussion forums have gone quiet, save for specific questions about course content or requests to correct errors in problem sets. By all means, check out every discussion forum, but don't expect all of them to host enlightening exchanges. Focus your efforts on following the most recently active threads and using key search words to locate potential colleagues with shared interests in your city and elsewhere in the world.

You should seek out courses that actively foster social interaction. For example, *Beyond Silicon Valley* emphasizes making connections with other people by offering course mentors and encouraging the formation of peer-to-peer learning groups. In such courses, you will much more likely encounter like-minded students who would love to study with you. One MOOC platform in particular, the NovoEd platform, is known for encouraging students to connect with one another. NovoEd hosts many business and entrepreneurship courses, often created by industry professionals, including courses like *Global Social Entrepreneurship, Technology Entrepreneurship*, and *Design Kit: The Course for Human-Centered Design.* Social entrepreneurship-focused organizations such as +Acumen, PhilanthropyU, IDEO, and the Center for Global Enterprise have developed these and other courses for NovoEd's platform, many of them taking advantage of NovoEd's group collaboration technology to help students form groups, share documents, and organize video chats and conferences.

In addition to the MOOC platforms themselves, you can find opportunities to form or join online learning communities at MOOCLab.club. For face-to-face connections, try MOOC Meetups, listed on Meetup.com for cities including Chicago, Beijing, Mexico City, Dhaka, Amsterdam, and Boston. Likewise, P2PU (short for Peer to Peer University) facilitates the creation of in-person learning circles. I also invite you to join the Facebook group I host for online business students. You can find the link on the *Don't Pay For Your MBA* book extras page (www.nopaymba. com/book-extras).

Exercise patience. It may take time and a number of failed attempts before you find a learning community that works for you. It's worth the time and effort, because you will find the connections you make a wonderfully rewarding experience, and not just in terms of furthering your career goals. You will make friends, receive a lot of support for your endeavors, and learn a lot that you can never get from watching online video lectures.

If you enjoy taking the initiative and wish to develop your leadership skills, try your hand at facilitating a learning community yourself. This can help you to ensure high-quality interactions. That's what Arjan did. It's also how Brandon, an American entrepreneur living in Japan, chose to study. Brandon organized a few of his contacts to take a set of business MOOCs as a group. The group met weekly at Brandon's office and gradually grew in size, as friends of friends joined in. As an American, Brandon could help clarify the professors' use of idiomatic expressions and provide context when the professors used examples drawn from American businesses. In turn, the Japanese learners in the group translated many concepts into the world of Japanese business, fostering understanding among both the local and the foreign participants in the group.

I found my own foray into learning communities richly rewarding. After two years of solo coursework, I yearned to connect with other learners in a more lasting way. In March 2015, I placed a tiny button on my website that said, "I'm forming a learning community. Will you join me?" Within a few days, fifty people had registered their email addresses and filled out a short application form. By July, the No-Pay MBA Network was up and running. I facilitated that learning group for nearly two years, during which time I organized mock negotiation exercises, planned courses for members to take together, brought in guest speakers, and introduced a lot of members to each other. Most rewarding, perhaps, was what I learned from the members of the group as they shared their ambitions, their goals, and their expertise.

The members of the community also benefited immensely from the shared experience. Kristof and Hillary, whose stories you read earlier in this book, met as two of the inaugural members of the No-Pay MBA Network. As Hillary says, "Members of the No-Pay MBA Network have become some of my closest friends and most trusted professional advisers/partners. I've also been able to co-create a mutually supportive mastermind group with some members as we all progress into similar career plans." Hillary has built an expansive network through her studies, not only in the No-Pay MBA Network but also in her volunteer work as a Course Catalyst mentor for several courses produced by +Acumen on the NovoEd platform. This opportunity arose when the course facilitators noticed Hillary's high level of engagement and mastery of the material. She has since gone on to join a more elite group of learning advocates, the +Acumen Corps, with an offer to serve as the Lead Editor of +Acumen's Yearbook. That role ties in nicely with Hillary's professional life as a publisher.

TIPS FOR FORMING AND FACILITATING A LEARNING GROUP

- Start with a course on the NovoEd platform that requires group work. For example, *Technology Entrepreneurship* asks you to use teamwork to identify ideal customers, determine their problems, and propose solutions.

- Set requirements for participation. You want to attract highly motivated and hardworking people who are very likely to complete the course in its entirety (those who have completed a MOOC before, have taken more than one course on the same topic, have signed up for a multicourse series, have paid for a verified certificate, etc.).

- Pay attention to time zone, and determine a group meeting time convenient to all participants. This can be tricky for international groups with students in the United States, China, and Timbuktu. Try out a scheduling app, such as Google Calendar or World Time Buddy.

- Take advantage of free project management tools such as Google Drive, Trello, and Google Hangouts. With Google Drive's file-sharing software, for example, you can create a group folder that everyone can easily access.

- Set goals for the group. Make these goals achievable, specific, and time-sensitive. For example, the group might set its sights on finishing all the requirements of a certain course, meeting a predetermined number of times, and/or creating a joint report or presentation, all within a specific time frame.

- Clarify the roles and responsibilities of each individual participant. Consider appointing individuals to specific tasks, such as scheduling and facilitating meetings, gauging participation, or, in the case of a final project, drafting various portions of the summary report.

- Find members through multiple channels, including the course discussion forum, MOOCLab.club, the No-Pay MBA Facebook group, LinkedIn, and others.

- Go easy on yourself. Facilitating a learning group can pose a lot of challenges, especially with members scattered across the globe and busy with a multitude of commitments. Use what you learn from your first experience to improve your next one.

As with all of the relationships in your life, you must consistently invest time building and nurturing the ones you form with other online learners. A one-minute investment in a "Hey, how are you doing?" email will keep the connection alive.

Create Your One-Hour-Per-Week Networking Plan

C hris Haroun, a Silicon Valley venture capitalist whose background includes working at such big-name finance and management consulting firms as Goldman Sachs, Citadel, and Accenture, frequently serves as a guest lecturer at Bay Area business schools, including Berkeley and Stanford. He also created one of the most popular business courses on the Udemy platform, *An Entire MBA in One Course*. In his live university classes Haroun often polls his students at the beginning of the semester, asking, "What if, for the next twenty weeks, you could do something that takes just one hour per week, and guarantee that you would get the job of your dreams? Raise your hand if you would do that thing." Inevitably, every hand shoots up. Who wouldn't spend just an hour per week during a single semester to land their dream job? And yet, most students get so caught up in class projects, assignments, and social obligations that they never spend a mere hour each week to move toward their career goal. Haroun's One-Hour-Per-Week Plan costs nothing to implement. You just invest one hour per week for twenty weeks conducting informational interviews (a form of networking—see Figure 6-2) and talking to individuals who not only provide information but turn into professional connections.

In *An Entire MBA in One Course*, Haroun tells students that anyone can replicate a valuable business school network by devoting one hour per week to making strategic use of networking platforms such as LinkedIn. Once again, social media meets six degrees of separation.

Figure 6-2

◆ **ADVISER'S CHALLENGE** ◆

INTERVIEW YOUR WAY
TO A WORLD-CLASS NETWORK

☐ **Review your hypotheses from Chapter 5 regarding industry, company, and role.** People who work in your target industries, companies, and roles can add both information and connections to your business education.

☐ **Make a list of six people you want to interview.** If you implement the six degrees of separation principle, you can put anyone, no matter how high up in an organization, on your target list. However, keep in mind that the top dog can seldom provide as much insight and help as much as the pack you run with. If possible, start with people you already know or have met. Use LinkedIn to identify other people in your "friend of a friend" network who work in your target companies, industries, or roles.

☐ **Compose a short message you can deliver to each person on your list, asking for an interview.** People will respond best to a single paragraph request that clearly states your reason for contacting them and asks for a brief conversation (thirty minutes ▼

at most) by phone, on social media, or in person. You want to make it easy for people to say yes. Always use the name of the person who recommended this connection. If you are making a cold call, LinkedIn can come to the rescue by allowing your target connection to learn about you before agreeing to a chat.

. . . .

❑ **Research your target.** A well-prepared interviewer gets the best results. Find out as much as you can about the person you want to interview. People respond more warmly to interviewers who have done their homework. You may want to prepare a few questions so that you feel comfortable kicking off the conversation.

. . . .

❑ **Allow the conversation to flow naturally.** If you have prepared a set of questions you want to ask, don't let that list derail an interesting conversation. Also, keep an eye on the clock, and make sure you respect the interviewee's busy schedule.

. . . .

❑ **Share your resume.** You can use all the feedback you can get to the way you present your nontraditional business education. DO NOT ask if the target's company is hiring or say that you are looking for a job, but DO ask how that person ended up in their current role. People like to talk about their own careers, especially the surprising ways they landed where they did.

. . . .

❑ **Ask for an introduction to another person.** Most people will give you names of people they like and admire or think can help you fill in your knowledge about their business.

. . . .

❑ **Say thank you.** People enjoy receiving a thank-you note for their time and generosity. Mention something personal you learned about the person. That will help cement a more lasting bond.

Informational interviewing expands your network, of course, but it also sets you up to return favors later in your career. Brian interviewed Julianne when he was researching jobs in entertainment production. That led him to Josh, who eventually hired Brian as an intern on a production crew for a network evening news program. Several years later, after Brian moved into a senior production role at the network, he got a call from Julianne, saying she had taken time off to raise her family and hoped Brian could introduce her to Josh. Networking works both ways.

Follow the Five Principles of Networking

Networking is part art, part science. While some people naturally make friends wherever they go and find it easy to ask for and grant favors, others of us must work at it. If you fall into the latter camp, as so many of us do, these five basic principles might make you more comfortable forging the connections you need:

1. **Offer help and support.** It's easy to forget the power of this variation of the Golden Rule. People help those who help them. When Arjan started his *Beyond Silicon Valley* study group, he didn't do it with purely selfish motives; he truly wanted to serve his community. If networking seems contrived or phony to you, try reframing the process by asking, "How might I help the people I want to meet?" As much as you need them, they need you. For more on this principle, take a look at Adam Grant's *Give and Take: Why Helping Others Drives Our Success.*
2. **Make networking a regular practice.** We talked about the One-Hour-Per-Week Plan. At least a couple of times each week, do

something (no matter how small) to grow or deepen your network, whether writing a note to a former classmate, sending an email to someone you'd like to meet, or adding information to your LinkedIn profile. In addition, keep jotting down new ideas for expanding your network. Don't restrict this practice to the early stages of your career; make it a lifetime habit.

3. **Play the long game.** Maintain a rich range of connections. As we saw with Brian and Julianne, you never know when a person higher up the ladder will become a peer or even a subordinate. Network at all levels and across a broad spectrum, even with people in far different industries, companies, and roles. Over the span of your work life, you may go from banker to baker to candlestick maker (and back again).

4. **Keep it real.** The Internet can feel like a cold and impersonal place, but you can pump life into it by treating your virtual interactions as you would those in your real life. Let your humanity rule your chats and conversations. It's another variation of the Golden Rule: Treat others as human beings, and they will return the favor. My network includes many people I have never met face-to-face, but who have nonetheless become trusted advisers, collaborators, and friends. When someone's work inspires you, reach out to let him or her know your feelings. Sure, you might not hear back, but you might end up making someone's day and forging a new connection to boot.

5. **Make honesty your number-one priority.** Honesty really is the best policy. All too often, folks create false online personae in an attempt to mask flaws and shortcomings or to disguise the fact that they are newbies with an incomplete business education or little experience in the workplace. This only builds a false impression that sooner or later will bite you in an uncomfortable

place. We've talked about first impressions. If it turns out that you have built yours on quicksand, it will end up doing more harm than good.

Michael Salmon, author of the book *Supernetworking: Reach the Right People, Build Your Career Network, and Land Your Dream Job*, practices what he preaches. His company, Salmon & Associates, specializes in consulting to financial advisers in major financial institutions. Clients and competitors consider him one of the foremost trainers and coaches in the field, but it didn't happen overnight. It took years of assiduous networking that began when he confided his ambition to get into the financial services industry with a second cousin who happened to work at Merrill Lynch. The cousin introduced Michael to his boss, upon whom Michael made such a favorable impression that she scheduled time for him to meet with her and two regional sales managers. That meeting led to several assignments with Merrill Lynch and opened doors to doing business with Morgan Stanley, Smith Barney, Bank of America, UBS, Wells Fargo, SunTrust, Credit Suisse, and others.

Was it a stroke of luck that launched Michael's successful career? Not by a long shot. "I figured out how to access the right people in those organizations and convince them that our programs would help them get better results," he says. "I now run exactly the sort of business I always wanted: I make good money, I love what I do, I'm happy 365 days a year, and because I give back as much as I get from others, I enjoy the rewards of unusually good karma. And it all started with that first conversation with a second cousin."

POINTS TO REMEMBER

1. Think strategically when you build your network of professional contacts; include a wide range of connections, from fellow business students to potential employers or investors.
2. Craft an honest online business persona that will make a great first impression on everyone who sees it.
3. Create and/or join supportive learning communities.
4. Use informational interviews to expand both your knowledge and your network of professional contacts.
5. Make networking a lifelong habit.

7

Deepen Your Expertise

Establishing Your
Professional Credibility

MARK gives himself a high-five as he leaves the meeting. He has just nailed a presentation to a group of senior managers at MedSync, the Fortune 500 medical technology company where he works. An accomplished engineer, Mark has always loved tinkering with devices and coming up with ideas that will make them more efficient. When he was promoted into a management role, heading a small team of engineers, he quickly realized that he needed to learn a lot more about the business side of his industry. A more efficient device would not make it to market unless it made bottom-line sense, and it wouldn't succeed unless customers fell in love with it. Thankfully, a MOOC-based business education, capped off by a set of data science courses, came to his rescue.

When Mark first dove into the world of online business education, he was looking for broad-based business knowledge that could bolster his career. He didn't expect to find data analysis so fascinating. Had he enrolled in a traditional MBA program, he might not even have stumbled onto the topic at all, because many MBA programs do not require their students to take it. However, the choose-your-own curriculum he had devised for himself led him to the Data Science Specialization from Johns Hopkins (on Coursera), a set of courses that included everything from a basic introduction to advanced techniques. Before long, Mark began looking at everything related to his work through the lens of data analysis, and everywhere he looked he saw opportunities for MedSync to use data to capture a competitive edge. When his personal list of data science projects grew longer than a page, he took a risk and invited his boss and a few other senior managers to a short meeting on a Friday afternoon. During a carefully orchestrated thirty-minute pitch, he built the business case for tackling three projects that would take advantage of data the company was already gathering. The result? The top brass asked Mark to lead a new product development initiative, using data on customer preferences to design profitable new products.

Many MBA programs offer students the opportunity to specialize by selecting an MBA concentration. As with a college major, a concentration builds deep expertise in a narrow realm of the business curriculum. To replicate this online, you will need to take several courses on the same topic, progressing through more difficult and advanced material. To advance your career, you must become an expert in something, and to become an expert you need to dive deeply into a particular area of business that can fuel your success. What area of expertise do you want to deepen?

Choose Your MBA Concentration

By now, you've studied the basics, developed fluency in the language of business, and practiced the basic business competencies. In addition to your coursework, you've also taken stock of your aptitudes, thought deeply about the kind of work you enjoy, developed a set of hypotheses about Career-Self Fit, conducted some informational interviews, and begun to build your network of professional contacts. Now it's time to develop your expertise in a narrower field of study, one that flows naturally from everything you've learned so far.

Before you commit, however, survey the MOOC platforms to look for sets of courses in your prospective concentration. Do you see multiple courses on your topic? Coursera's multicourse Specializations fit the bill; likewise edX offers a set of MicroMasters programs. Even if the MOOC platforms haven't packaged a set of courses for you, you still want to find at least four to six more advanced courses related to your concentration. Fewer may indicate too narrow a focus. In Mark's area of concentration, for example, Coursera offers dozens of courses on data analysis, from the University of California's *Data Visualization with Tableau* to the University of Illinois's *Exploring and Producing Data for Business Decision Making* and Duke University's *Master Data Analysis in Excel.*

If you find few courses on your topic, you may need to exercise a little flexibility. Some years ago, one of my fellow MOOC business students reached out to ask for advice on how to structure a concentration in hospital administration. However, she could find very few courses on that specific topic, and most of them were introductory. I advised her to take a more flexible approach to gaining the expertise she needed, perhaps specializing in supply chain management or organizational development and seeking courses on management that seemed especially well-suited to the medical field, perhaps even supplementing her online education with a few carefully chosen in-person workshops or short courses.

Beyond finding enough material to deepen your expertise, you want to make sure that you enjoy the work and can see its ready application to your career needs. At this stage you are still testing your hypotheses. You may plunge into a series of courses only to find the material boring or of little practical use on the job. Fortunately, you have not spent a fortune or wasted a whole year making that mistake. You can rethink and refocus in a heartbeat.

As the MOOC platforms develop new university partnerships and expand their reach, they will continue branching out into new subject areas. Even if you don't find a lot of options in a particular area of interest today, don't give up. You may be at the beginning of a brand-new and exciting field. Ten years ago no one was talking about Big Data. Now, it's all the rage.

Some of the subject areas that currently offer the widest range of courses include:

- Entrepreneurship, including social entrepreneurship
- Marketing, especially digital marketing
- Management and leadership
- Strategy and innovation
- Data analysis
- Finance

Feel free to do what the hopeful hospital administrator did and develop a concentration that works for you. Also consider giving your concentration a unique title that captures your particular area of interest. For example, Jerome, whom we met in Chapter 4, called his concentration Social Sector Leadership; Hillary, who first appeared in Chapter 1, pursued Impact Entrepreneurship and Innovation; and Mark selected Data Science and Strategy. With a little imagination they all found courses that suited their needs.

Set Up a Professional Practice

You've identified a concentration, found advanced coursework, and begun studying at an advanced level. Now you need to apply your developing skills in a real-world setting. At this point, however, you will not be engaging in a trial run, you'll be doing it live and in-person. It's like moving beyond practicing your legal skills in a mock trial and arguing a case in court. You might undertake a special project in the company where you currently work, as Mark did, or you might land a temporary assignment in the form of a short-term consultancy or internship. You might even dip your toe into the entrepreneurial shark tank. Look for opportunities in companies and organizations where you can actually do marketing, data analysis, management consulting, entrepreneurship, etc.

Mark convinced management that he was ready to practice what he had learned as the leader of a new data analysis project. If you see an opportunity to take on a special project at work, propose the idea to your supervisor. Or, better yet, do what Mark did and invite senior leadership to a pitch meeting at which you present ideas that could benefit the company. For him, pitching at work not only benefited his employer, it added a valuable line to his professional resume. If you don't feel confident proposing a pitch meeting at your place of work, you might use one of your learning laboratories to create a similar experience.

Some learners create their own internships by offering their skills pro bono as independent consultants. A small business owner may never have thought about working with nonpaid helpers but would love to improve efficiency or sell more widgets. And you don't have to quit your day job to satisfy your entrepreneurial appetite. People "moonlight" all the time, whether holding down two jobs to make ends meet or operating a small business after work and on weekends for both fun and profit.

Many advanced coursework packages include a final project. For example, if you take the *Business Strategy Specialization* from the University of Virginia on Coursera, the last assignment in the final course in the series asks that you use all the strategic analysis techniques you've studied to create a strategy report for a company of your choosing. If the advanced coursework you choose includes such a project, you won't need to structure your final project yourself. Still, even for a structured class project, you should consider pairing up with a company that could benefit from your skills. For example, the *Marketing Mix Implementation Specialization* from IE Business School, also on Coursera, includes a final project using Tesla Motors as a case study. Once you've worked through marketing and distribution channels, advertising, PR, and communications budgeting for the Tesla case, you will likely want to take those same skills to a company that can benefit from your services. Not only will this strengthen your educational experience, it will allow you to build bridges to your chosen industry, not to mention adding an important line to your resume.

Traditional MBA programs quite often include short-term consulting projects. Students typically complete these projects in groups, as part of class assignments during the regular semester, through extracurricular clubs, or on field trips. You can replicate that experience by seizing an incredible (and completely free) opportunity offered to independent business students by the Center for Global Enterprise (CGE), a nonprofit research institute that studies contemporary global corporations and offers courses and experiences that teach key management skills to future business leaders. In addition to offering courses on the NovoEd platform,

CGE periodically organizes a program called the Alpha Team, which mimics the consultancies you might find in traditional business programs. CGE recruits globally for the Alpha Team, involving independent learners, traditional business students enrolled in MBA programs, and even business professors. Teams perform consulting projects for companies around the world. One recent Alpha Team created a suite of online management courses for the Nigerian jobs platform Jobberman. A previous Alpha Team developed a strategic plan for Rasello, a Tanzanian software firm. Students who have participated in the Alpha Team initiative have found it a truly professional experience. They enjoy their relationships with highly engaged and knowledgeable mentors and enthusiastic fellow students who bring a wealth of experience to a project. Best of all, perhaps, they expand their resumes and add terrific new connections to their networks.

A program like the Alpha Team can only accommodate a limited number of students at a time, but an intrepid student could easily set up his or her own short-term, pro bono consulting gig. Carrie, who studied business at George Washington University, joined an independent consulting club, where students banded together to serve clients in the Washington, D.C., area. When the time came for Carrie to organize a project, she drew on her prior background in textile arts and offered her team's help to an arts organization in D.C. As it turned out, leaders of the organization had thought about hiring a consulting firm to help overhaul its membership structure, but could not afford to hire high-priced consultants. Carrie's club offered the perfect solution. Her team of fellow business students drafted a proposal and a contract, which the arts organization quickly accepted. At the end of the engagement, the organization adopted the student consulting team's recommendation to institute a new membership structure. Carrie describes this experience as one of the highlights of business school. Think about organizing an extracurricular consulting club that can give a team of fellow online students some real-world business experience with pro bono consulting. Draw from your learning group and approach the project in a professional manner, clearly defining the assignment, structuring it around specific deliverables and deadlines, managing your time effectively, and delivering high-caliber results on time and at no cost to your client.

Figure 7-1

▶ **ADVISER'S CHALLENGE** ◀

COMPLETE A CULMINATION PROJECT

☐ **Decide whether to form/join a team or fly solo.** If you belong to a learning group, suggest that members of the group tackle a final project where they can test their knowledge and skills in the real world. Otherwise, search your network for teammates. Learners with a strong independent streak might prefer striking out on their own.

☐ **Determine the specific services you will offer potential clients.** Of course, you will draw from your area of concentration. Think in terms of fulfilling real needs and solving real problems. In some cases, a team might span several diverse disciplines, including your concentration (say, finance) and other key areas where a small business owner might need help, from outsourcing to marketing/sales.

☐ **Target three organizations that could benefit from your services.** Even if you do not currently hold a job in your chosen industry, you may have formed a relationship with a particular company already. Put it on your target list. But also look for two or three other organizations where you can see a win/win opportunity: The company benefits from your work, and you extend your network. Caution: You will enjoy more success with smaller outfits (nonprofits, startups, and family businesses) because the Fortune 1000 will generally prefer a big, established consulting company.

....

☐ **Prepare your pitch.** You should tailor your presentation to the particular nature and needs of each organization on your target list. How can you best package your services in a way that will catch their attention? Again, focus on specific needs/solutions. Stress concrete results. For example, suppose you have targeted a not-for-profit organization that plans to launch a major fund-raising campaign. Your pitch might go something like this:

Dear Director of Capital Funding,

I am an independent student currently taking advanced MBA-level courses in marketing communications. I am looking for an opportunity to apply my professional skills with a short-term, pro bono *consulting project. I admire the commitment Bridges has made to help formerly incarcerated inmates make successful transitions back into society and would love to help design effective messaging for your forthcoming Capital Funding Project. Reaching your $1,000,000 goal will require carefully crafted marketing communications to support a low or no cost public relations and publicity campaign. I have attached examples of press releases and online promotions I have created for class assignments.*

Thank you for considering this offer. I hope we can arrange a one-hour meeting, so I can gather the information I need to make a formal proposal for helping Bridges reach its goal.

☐ **Structure the work around deliverables and deadlines.** You may have done coursework in project management. If not, you might want to brush up with a MOOC on the subject. In any event, you must focus on the concrete work product you will deliver on time and on budget. Clients want to see tangible results with no surprise costs. Even though the client will not pay for your services, you should deliver high-value results. If you see the schedule slipping, make sure you inform the client immediately and agree on a new deadline for the deliverable.

☐ **Deliver outstanding, professional quality work.** How would you behave if your career depended on fulfilling this assignment? Act like a consulting pro. You may be writing press releases for your client on your laptop while lounging on the couch in your bathrobe, but you want your contacts at the client organization to picture you in impeccable business attire, seated in front of a 27-inch iMac. Your professional image matters, even when the work is not for pay.

Learn by the Light of the Moon

If you feel 100 percent certain you will never want to work for yourself, feel free to skip this section. Before you do that, however, I must tell you that a tremendous number of the self-directed learners that I know (including those described in Chapter 1) possess a dominant entrepreneurial gene. Many of these budding entrepreneurs satisfy their entrepreneurial hunger by starting a business of their own, moonlighting while working for someone else, or convincing their employer to sponsor an entrepreneurial initiative. Take a few minutes to consider what you might learn if you design an entrepreneurial Culmination Project (see Figure 7-1).

I did that with the No-Pay MBA Network (see Chapter 6). It began as a moonlighting initiative that provided the perfect culmination to my independent studies. As any business owner will attest, starting and running your own venture gives you a perspective on business that no other experience can match. My own initiative taught me a lot about business and myself that I would have gotten no other way. I had to think about everything a new business owner must ponder: product design and branding, marketing communication, managing growth, and adding staff (starting with a personal assistant who converted her own moonlighting experiment into a successful career). I urge every reader to do something on the side (or at night and on the weekends) that lets you learn big while betting small.

MOOC student Brandi, the marketer you met in Chapter 6, did just that. While taking courses as part of her MOOC business education, she seized the opportunity to participate in an employer-paid professional training course. After her MOOC experience gave her some insight into what constitutes a good course, Brandi contacted the course instructors with some constructive feedback. The instructors found her insights so helpful that they ended up offering her a limited consulting gig to help reshape some of the training company's offerings. Though she had contemplated doing a bit of consulting on the side, she had not expected such a perfect opportunity to fall in her lap. The gig nicely combined her background in marketing with her more recent MOOC-based training on strategy. With that one client on her resume, Brandi went on to set up a steady moonlighting practice, offering herself as an expert on brand strategy.

If you like the idea of moonlighting, think about taking or retaking Steve Blank's course *How to Build a Startup*. As Blank suggests in the course, you can start out by interviewing your prospective customers to discover the problems your business can solve. There's no point in starting a business, even one on the side, if you cannot solve real problems and deliver real results. What, exactly, will you offer? How will you package your product or services? Can you easily finance the operation until it turns a profit? Make sure you structure the operation in a way that allows you to get the most out of the experience. Carefully manage, monitor, and learn from the experience. Once you've determined what you can do for your customers, register your business, select an accounting system, and set up a bank account. All of these activities enable you to test-drive your competence with a wide range of business disciplines. You may end up taking what you have learned to your current or future employer, or you might even turn moonlight into daylight, running your own business full-time.

Document and Display Your Achievements

You will never reap the full benefits of your self-directed business education if you do not communicate it clearly and compellingly. Once you have completed some advanced coursework, tested your expertise in at least one real-world situation, and performed some professional-caliber work, your next step is to present proof of your business skills and acumen with a high-quality portfolio. Think of your portfolio as a professional calling card you can share with a current or prospective employer, potential clients and customers, and investors.

This brings us back to the motto: "Show, don't tell." You need to put your accomplishments *on the page*, physically and/or electronically. If you were a graphic designer, a photographer, or even a software designer, you wouldn't simply describe your work; you would submit impressive examples of it. When you picture the audience for your business portfolio, imagine someone who has seen a thousand others and will look at yours with a skeptical eye. Will your portfolio impress the hard-nosed CEO of a Fortune 100 company? You can create an impressive portfolio online using LinkedIn, your personal/professional website, or a portfolio website such as Pathbrite. To showcase my education, I built a portfolio feature into my blog site, which I made available for other MOOC students to use. You can register for a free portfolio at www.NoPayMBA.com/portfolio.

These days, even traditional colleges and universities recognize the value of e-portfolios, encouraging (or even requiring) students to keep building one as they progress with their studies. For example, the entire University of California system now connects students to Portfolium, a company that partners with colleges and universities to help students show what they have accomplished. Portfolium's mission is to "help every student meet their full potential by integrating learning with career management in an open and connected network that makes it easier to discover, prepare, and qualify for the most relevant career opportunities."[1] If you've structured your Culmination Project properly (see Figure 7-1), you should come away from it with an accessible, shareable product that represents your best work. This could include a written report, a polished slide deck, or a video of a polished presentation. Add any finished work products from other courses you've taken or even from your current job or an entrepreneurial side project.

Pay attention to the organization of your portfolio (take the Adviser's Challenge in Figure 7-2). A good one tells your story, presenting you as an interesting and accomplished professional and leaving the reader wanting to know more. Replace long-winded blocks of text with bulleted lists, concise summaries, and informative graphics. Marketing guru and bestselling author Seth Godin offers a free downloadable e-booklet called *Really Bad PowerPoint (and How to Avoid It)*. In this short book, Godin outlines the essential rules for effective communication, which apply to all media. Download a copy and treat it as gospel when putting together your portfolio.

I've seen too many portfolios that look like someone threw a five-course Italian meal at a wall. The jumble of information obscures all of the delectable dishes. Once, a reader of the No-Pay MBA blog sent me a link to a personal site where he had uploaded over thirty MOOC certificates. "What do you think?" he proudly asked. I didn't know what to think. He had certainly done a lot of work, and I'm sure he had learned a thing or two—but *what*, exactly? Make sure your portfolio tells a coherent story. You wouldn't submit a pile of random, out-of-order chapters to an editor and call it a novel. Neither should you proffer two dozen MOOC certificates as the only evidence of your business education. That's just a transcript. Sometimes you need a transcript, of course, but a transcript does not tell a reader who you are, where you've been, and where you're going. My own college transcript includes elective credits for swimming and modern dance, alongside courses in statistics and political theory. While I still love dancing and swimming, I have yet to apply for a job that requires me to pirouette or swim the butterfly.

Think of your portfolio as a novel. You, the main character, progress through many adventures. A good novel highlights those adventures in a way that attracts and holds a reader's interest. Most readers would put down a novel that detailed everything you've ever done in chronological order: "I was born on August 16, 1988, then I went to kindergarten, then I ate lunch, then I went to bed, then I got up and went to high school, then I blah, blah, blah. . . ." Like an engrossing novel, your portfolio should highlight only the most interesting and compelling details, those that advance the plot toward a satisfying conclusion: a promotion, a new job, or a business startup. Do not confuse a portfolio with a resume. A resume merely serves as jacket-flap copy for your novel. In Chapter 8, we'll look closely at how you can most effectively incorporate your self-directed business education into your resume.

Figure 7-2

> ▶ **ADVISER'S CHALLENGE** ◀
>
> ## BUILD YOUR DIGITAL PORTFOLIO
>
> ☐ **Craft your key message.** While it is tempting when creating a portfolio to start by choosing which portfolio platform you will use and then uploading materials, I suggest you start instead by thinking about what message you would like your portfolio to convey. You could even think of your key message as a mission statement, a single sentence that summarizes where you have arrived as a result of your business education and where you want it to take you next. For example, Mark might state his mission this way: "I am an accomplished data analysis professional seeking to apply my skills in the marketing department of a major corporation." This mission statement doesn't need to be written anywhere in your portfolio, but it will guide the selection and organization of elements you include in it. ▼

❏ **Assemble the elements.** You want to display the best examples of your work to date. Identify tangible work products that you have produced, either on-the-job, during internships, or as a result of your Culmination Project. These might include written reports, blog posts or articles written by or about you, video presentations, slide decks, your website, or anything else that you can deliver to your target audience electronically or in-person. Make sure your examples tie closely to your mission statement, emphasizing your specific skills and your application of those skills. For example, Mark would not put a video of the ham radio he built in high school in a portfolio aimed at landing a job in data analysis.

❏ **Get permission to share elements owned by someone else.** As a rule, any work product created for an employer belongs to that organization, and you must get their written permission to use it in your portfolio. Companies fiercely protect their intellectual property and often require employees to sign nondisclosure agreements. If you cannot obtain written permission to share a work product, ask your employer for testimonials from management about the quality of that work. For example, while Mark did not even try to persuade his boss to let him share his presentation to management, he did get him to write a half-page testimonial about the fact that Mark's presentation eventually led to the development of many new products for MedSync.

❏ **Choose a display location.** You can enable access to your portfolio many different ways. Of course, you can print it up just as an artist would do, but in this age of digital communication, you should probably build your portfolio online. In a pinch, someone with few web creation skills can use simple tools such as WordPress, SquareSpace, and Google Sites. LinkedIn, About.me, and Strikingly.com also offer excellent options. Portfolium, Pathbrite, and Foliotek provide a good alternative for academic portfolios, but you might consider using the portfolio feature on NoPayMBA. com, designed specifically for MOOC business students. Mark not only built his own website with links to his major work products, he maintained a constant presence on LinkedIn and created a portfolio on NoPayMBA.com (with links to the projects on his personal site).

☐ **Make it attractive.** You may not be the world's greatest artist, but that should not stop you from making your portfolio look visually appealing. Avoid large blocks of text in favor of easily digestible images and short bullets that will keep your reader from falling asleep while browsing your portfolio. Use images to convey your message more powerfully. For example, Mark might have relied on his friend Greg, a graphic designer, to help him create an informative graphic that captured the essence of his presentation to management.

☐ **Get feedback.** Once you have made your portfolio as complete and well organized as possible, share it with folks in your network. Try to include someone with a background in graphics, a writer, a peer, a mentor, a professor, and anyone else who can give you an honest opinion from a professional perspective. Welcome feedback, even if you disagree with it.

☐ **Continue to grow your portfolio.** Keep updating your portfolio, adding new items, deleting ones that have become irrelevant, and rebuilding it from scratch if your mission changes. If Mark decides to move out of the medical field and into international consulting to not-for-profit organizations, he might keep some items, discard many others, and reorganize everything under a new banner: "I am an independent data analysis consultant seeking not-for-profit clients in Europe and Asia."

Always present yourself and your work professionally. In her forthcoming book *Excuse Me: The Survival Guide to Modern Business Etiquette*, author Rosanne Thomas tells a funny but enlightening story about HR director Mary, who was interviewing candidates for a key position.

> Chloe had the right skill set but her appearance was alarming. A snake tattoo coiled up her arm to her neck, in homage, she said, to her pet snake, "Rumplesnakeskin." She had multiple piercings in her ears, and wore a tank top sans bra and flip-flops with glittery blue nail polish on her toes. But Chloe was the best of the lot. So Mary offered her the job on one condition: that she come to work appropriately dressed for a conservative insurance company.

> First thing Monday morning, Mary gets a call from her boss. "May I see you in my office? Now!" he shouts, with unmistakable anger in his voice. Mary rushes to his office and sees Chloe sitting demurely outside his door, dressed in what Mary surmises is her version of conservative: a hot pink suit with a plunging neckline and micro-mini skirt, six inch stiletto heels, heavy gold chains and bracelets, extreme makeup, and of course, Rumplesnakeskin in plain sight.

Your ability to do the work won't guarantee a job offer. Like it or not, appearances do matter. And they matter in everything you do, whether you're showing up on the first day of a new job, pitching your services as a pro bono consultant, or displaying your work in a digital portfolio.

POINTS TO REMEMBER

1. Choose and label your MBA concentration, making sure that you can find at least four to six courses on that subject.
2. Complete a Culmination Project in which you apply your skills in a professional setting.
3. Consider a moonlighting venture as your Culmination Project.
4. Build an online portfolio where you professionally display your very best work.

8

Graduate to the Next Level

Using Your Self-Directed Business Education to Advance Your Career

JORIS'S interests range far and wide. He loves learning something about everything, from the names of rare plants and animals to graphic design. As a high school student, the young Dutchman developed a passion for science, but when he went to college, he decided that he didn't want to major in a purely technical field, so he picked industrial design. While still an undergraduate, he took on an ideal side project for someone who loves learning something new every day: He helped develop a new curriculum for the Scouting Nederland, which coordinates about 1,000 Dutch youth scouting groups. Joris found this work so engrossing that he decided to enroll in a master's degree program where he would study educational science, with a postgraduate diploma in library science thrown in for good measure—a perfect combination for someone who likes to dabble in a variety of subjects.

While in graduate school, Joris witnessed the dawn of the MOOC revolution and, not surprisingly, he fell in love with online learning. Suddenly, he no longer needed to limit his studies to a restrictive degree track. Now he could stay in grad school and still pursue the equivalent of an MBA. Oh, and he would take a little computer science coursework on the side. As graduation approached, Joris began to think seriously about life in the real world. What sort of career would make him happy? Thinking hard about his long-range future, he couldn't picture himself as a teacher or librarian. How about strategic consulting? It was his favorite business subject. Wouldn't that field offer new challenges every day? Hoping to impress target employers, Joris began weaving together all the educational patches he had collected into an attractive quilt. As you prepare to transition from studenthood, you too will need to compile a compelling story from your unique set of life, work, and online learning experiences.

Polish Your Credentials

M-B-A. Those three letters alone tell a powerful story. Many people hear someone say "MBA" and immediately think "smart, motivated, business-minded, professional." Your credentials need to inspire similar thoughts in the minds of those with whom you share them. We've already talked about finding Career-Self Fit, building a professional portfolio, and making a great first impression. Now we'll turn our attention to validating your credentials, carving out a thought leadership niche, thinking like a marketer, and acing every career-related interview.

Readers of the No-Pay MBA blog often ask me, "Without a degree to show for my efforts, will people take my self-directed business education seriously?" The answer begins with putting yourself in the shoes of a boss, a potential employer, or an investor. What sort of credentials will they want to examine? What will impress them the most? Bear in mind the bottom line for anyone looking to hire, promote, or invest in you: "Will this person succeed in this role?" An effective credential demonstrates that your business education was real, rigorous, and reputable. It may take the form of a diploma from a top-ten business school, but don't assume that an old-fashioned sheepskin is the only thing that counts in today's world of work. Consider other strong credentials, such as MOOC certificates and the *bona fides* that come from hard-won experience.

Imagine that you are an executive looking for someone to help you with a corporate merger or acquisition. As Christian Terwiesch, professor at the Wharton School of Business, once told me, "[Formal] certification is really only needed if you have studied for a long time and you haven't deployed these skills. If you study a new skill and then deploy it the next day, I don't need to certify you anymore," he said. "You can just write on your CV how you've completed a successful merger or acquisition. I don't need to write you a certificate that you've studied it. You actually are self-certified for having been successful on the job."[1]

Ideally, you can offer both kinds of proof. In any event, you want to amass a set of credentials that say, unambiguously, "I've prepared myself to do this job and to do it exceptionally well." Treat your credentials as signals you send to the world. A branch of economics pioneered by Michael Spence explores the role of "signaling" in the job market.[2] According to Spence and his colleagues, a credential's most important function is to send a signal about a person's capabilities. Let's suppose that the National Electronics Importers (NEI) advertises for a new supply chain manager and says "the ideal candidate should possess an MBA or the equivalent." NEI is basically saying, "This is what we think we would like to see in a candidate. What do *you* have to offer?" You won't get an interview, much less the job, unless you send the right signal to this prospective employer. The right signal could be a certificate from Coursera, relevant on-the-job experience (you managed inventory at Best Buy for three summers), or (best of all) a combination of the two.

You may know in your heart that you will succeed in a certain position, but you must provide clear and compelling evidence that you are capable of meeting *other people's standards*. Having been admitted to a university and earning a degree does that trick. But so does proof that you landed and held a job in the past, a glowing letter of recommendation, a certificate from a brick-and-mortar or online school, an award for excellence, or anything you have published in a reputable publication. References, both written and verbal, make excellent credentials. Ask your manager at Best Buy to write you a strong recommendation, or at the very least make sure he agrees to let you list his name as a reference on your resume. Ditto for internships, volunteer positions, and pro bono work. Keep in mind that job recruiters unanimously agree that work experience trumps every other credential (except in fields with legal requirements for degrees, such as law and medicine).

Also bear in mind that credentials in emerging fields and industries, such as data analysis and digital marketing, often come from industry players rather than universities. For anyone hiring recruits in such fields, credentials from leading companies (e.g., HubSpot Inbound Marketer, Salesforce Administrator, and Hadoop Developer) may work better magic than a degree on the wall. For example, Willow found that certification from the software company Salesforce sent the best possible signal to prospective employers in her industry. Her demonstrated mastery of the popular Salesforce software, coupled with a resume showing steady advancement at the marketing firm where she worked, put just the right polish on her credentials. The Adviser's Challenge in Figure 8-1 will get you started putting together your own package of credentials.

Figure 8-1

► ADVISER'S CHALLENGE ◄

SHOOT FOR THE STARS

☐ **List everything you can think of that demonstrates your skills and reliability.** This might include references from past and present employers, endorsements from teachers and counselors, credentials for coursework (conventional and online learning), degrees you've earned in any subject (not just business), documents you've published, and anything else that provides external validation. Obviously, a sheepskin qualifies, but so do certificates, letters, awards, and any other tangible proof you can share online or on paper.

☐ **Next, star any item on your list that represents a concrete credential or refers to an impressive accomplishment.** If you have completed a short course at Harvard, star it. Do the same if you earned a promotion at any job. Add anything else that shows you are able to succeed by the standards of others, such as an article you published in a respected industry publication. Of course, star any written recommendations from current or former employers.

☐ **Look for gaps in your credentials.** If your list includes fewer than six stars, you will want to add several more as soon as possible. Make sure you can realistically accomplish each goal in a reasonable amount of time.

☐ **Design a strategy for filling the star gaps.** You should think about specific ways you can accomplish the goals on your list. Name specific courses on specific platforms or specific jobs at specific companies. MOOC certificates can fill in some of the gaps, but rather than buying a certificate for every course you ▼

take, choose a few from which you think you will get the most mileage. Seek written recommendations from colleagues, clients, and supervisors who can vouch for you.

Course series offer an excellent option for anyone's credentialing strategy. By completing several related courses, you demonstrate your motivation, your commitment to the subject, and your expanding knowledge and skills. For example, Mark earned a certificate indicating successful completion of the ten-course series *Data Science Specialization* from Johns Hopkins University, a much more impressive credential than a certificate of completion for a single course, *Intro to Data Science.* Keep an eye out for new forms of credentials, too. In 2016, the MOOC platform edX announced a slate of new MicroMasters programs. As the name suggests, these courses result in a credential short of a formal master's degree but do indicate academic rigor and a deep commitment to the subject.

When it comes to polishing your credentials, having a few big names on your resume can also work to your advantage. Like it or not, people are impressed by an association with Harvard, Stanford, and other big-name business schools. The same holds true for Apple or General Electric or Procter & Gamble. You may not be able get a credential from a Fortune 100 company, but you can obtain impressive experience from any widely recognizable organization. In the world of education, both Wharton and the Harvard Business School offer online courses as well as on-campus workshops for business professionals. MIT's entrepreneurship boot camp has launched many careers over its short history. Hillary, whose story has appeared throughout this book, found value in earning a Certificate in Social Sector Leadership from the University of California Berkeley Haas School of Business. This certificate played an important role in her credentialing strategy because it came from a well-known university—and it did not cost her a penny. Joris used a similar strategy, earning certificates from both Harvard Business School's online platform, HBX, and from the University of Pennsylvania's School of Social Policy and Practice. These short, relatively inexpensive credential-bearing programs allowed Joris to include the names of two brand-name institutions on his resume.

I would not be doing my job as your MOOC MBA Adviser if I did not say that there's nothing wrong with signing up for a traditional MBA education, provided you have done your due diligence. In Chapter 1 we talked about Explorers who seek to take the MBA for a test-drive. Some of these Explorers conclude that they really should buy the car (i.e., take the traditional route to an MBA). For example, Jessamine, who started her career in book publishing, decided through the course of her independent business studies that she wanted to go into management consulting and work her way into upper-level management at a large company. Her research into the companies and roles on her short list convinced her that only an old-fashioned master's degree would make the transition possible. She used what she had learned in a MOOC on financial valuation to determine that a one-year European MBA program would yield a positive return within a two- or three-year time horizon. If you find, as a result of all of your studies, personal reflection, and research, that an MBA degree is your best bet, go for it.

Demonstrate Thought Leadership

You can powerfully strengthen your personal brand by demonstrating "thought leadership." Thought leaders gain respect by taking a fresh and often unexpected perspective on a particular subject. You don't need to be a household name to be a thought leader (though the most successful thought leaders often do become famous). As professor Barbara Oakley points out in the MOOC course *Learning How to Learn*, new insights in science and other fields often come from people who are new to the discipline, including both young people and people initially trained in some other subject.

You may never have heard of Roger Connors, but he spent twenty-five years establishing himself as the number-one thought leader on the subject of accountability. Author of the New York Times bestseller *The Oz Principle*, he founded Partners in Leadership, a global consulting company that has trained over a million people to take accountability for results. Whether or not you shoot for fame, I recommend that you develop at least a modest catalog of material that makes your expertise visible to the world. The easiest way to start sharing your ideas and expertise is by blogging. If you don't want to set up your own website, consider using Medium, a blogging platform specifically designed to house thought leadership pieces. LinkedIn offers another good option for sharing your thoughts easily and quickly. While you might want to repost any articles you write to Facebook and other social media sites, I do not recommend Facebook as a primary outlet for sharing your thoughts. Facebook does not lend itself to building a catalog of articles for perusal by current or prospective employers or potential investors. (Not to mention, you probably do not want people you hope to impress professionally digging deep into your personal account.)

Before you hit "publish," keep in mind that even Hemingway needed a good editor. The number-one enemy of self-publishing is poor quality. You can learn to serve as your own editor, or you can ask a friend or colleague to lend you her expertise with the English language. Do not rely solely on autocorrect and spell-checkers to catch embarrassing mistakes, egregious spelling and grammar errors, or logical lapses. I once posted a blog article titled "5 Reasons I'm Okay with Not Getting a Degree." Soon after the post went live, a reader responded, "I think you left out a key word in point number 3." Turns out I had written, "The content of an MBA is valuable with or with the degree," rather than "with or without the degree."

If you enjoy blogging, you might expand your thought leadership strategy into other media, such as podcasting, writing articles for external publications, or curating content through social media. You might also take a look at Karen Nelson-Field's book *Viral Marketing: The Science of Sharing.* It and other books on the subject show you how to think and act as a marketer, reaching more people with messages that are relevant to them. Keep in mind that the way to establish yourself as an authoritative thought leader is to build trust with your audience by consistently providing high-quality, thought-provoking, helpful content.

Like any successful marketer, you need to carve out a unique, somewhat narrow niche. For example, do not try to become a thought leader on a far-ranging, overcrowded field such as "leadership" or "marketing." Rather, look for a small subset where you really can become a leading-edge expert on the subject. Roger Connors did it with "accountability," a distinct subset of "leadership."

When Joris started blogging, he drew on his unique experience with MOOCs, his interest in business strategy, and his passion for education. His published articles included such titles as "3 Things I Learned from Completing 60 MOOCs in 10 Months" and "The Future of Education: A School in 2025." Finding a niche where you can amass knowledge and share meaningful, important, and helpful insight can help you chart your professional path, as discussed in Chapter 5. Look into your heart, tap your passion, and devote time to learning and communicating something new.

The niche approach also applies to your audience. Do you want to beam your messages to the whole World Wide Web indiscriminately, or can you target a subset that really wants and needs to hear what you have to say? Look for publications in the field where you want to become a thought leader. Post reactions, reviews, and comments that contribute to the discussion of an issue that excites people in that field. Not only will you add value to the conversation, you may gain fans and friends and followers who like and respect your ideas.

Market, Market, Market

Luke, a psychiatrist, didn't begin his MOOC adventure with a career transition in mind. He just wanted to learn a bit about business. However, as he was taking courses on design thinking and entrepreneurship, he fell in love with the idea of customer-centered design. "What would mental health care look like," he wondered, "if we delivered it from the perspective of the *patient*, not the pharmaceutical company or even the doctor?" He soon discovered several new companies hard at work answering just that question.

Two in particular attracted his attention. Both were developing smartphone apps capable of gathering data, offering customized care recommendations, and connecting patients to experts who could provide on-demand attention. "Yes," Luke thought, "this can make a huge difference in people's lives. I would love to work for one of these companies." But having worked only in big, bureaucratic health systems, he felt unsure about convincing a startup tech company that he would make a valuable hire.

Luke addressed that issue by overhauling his LinkedIn profile to emphasize his independent business studies, as well as some modest entrepreneurial efforts he had undertaken to reduce inefficiency in the hospital where he currently worked. Next, he tweaked his resume and prepared cover letters detailing how his medical background, coupled with his newfound passion for user-centered design, would bring tremendous value to a tech startup focused on mental health. Finally, he reached out through his network of connections to obtain some important introductions. Luke soon found himself interviewing with two of the hottest startups in the emerging field of personalized mental health services.

To paraphrase the old real estate adage, career advancement depends on three things: marketing, marketing, and marketing. By adopting his customer's/potential employer's perspective, Luke figured out how to present himself as an ideal job candidate. Throughout your pursuit of your MOOC-based MBA, you have been wearing your learner's cap. Now it's time to replace it with your marketer's hat.

Any introductory marketing course would stress a few key concepts you should understand before you march into an interview with your boss, a potential employer, or a would-be investor. First, focus on *customer value*. Success in any marketing campaign depends on giving customers what they really need and want. To do that, you must put yourself in the customer's shoes. Luke did it by pondering a startup's main goals and then displaying how his education, work experience, and keen motivation could help the fledgling company achieve those goals. Then he thought about his competition for the job. Who else will most likely apply for the same niche? What gifts will they bring to the party? Will you find yourself competing with folks who hold Ivy League MBAs, or will you run up against a panel full of engineers? To answer those questions, you need to establish what marketers call *points of parity*. What makes you similar to the competition? How will you deliver as much, if not more, value to the customer? Then you must think about *differentiation*. What makes you stand out from the pack? What can you offer that your rivals can't match?

It helps to use a little imagination to answer these questions. Luke received callbacks from both prospective employers because he had assembled a unique combination of medical background and business savvy. One of the recruiters told Luke that she admired the drive he displayed when he took an unconventional path to acquire the business education he needed. Her company prized that sort of entrepreneurialism. As Luke discovered, it pays to present your unconventional approach to your education as a positive point of differentiation. Other candidates applying for the product development job may have outmatched Luke in terms of design experience, but none came close to his high-energy determination to succeed in this emerging field, and very few were likely to possess his deep knowledge of medicine. Think of it this way: Most of your competitors will have taken the well-traveled path to obtain the credentials they need to win a promotion, land a new job, or attract an investor. But you have taken the less-traveled path, one that requires more creativity, perseverance, and self-discipline. On your unique path you have learned a few things you seldom pick up in a conventional classroom: an entrepreneurial spirit, a high level of motivation, an abundance of creativity, cost-consciousness, practicality, critical thinking, resourcefulness, follow-through, and fierce independence. Think deeply about your points of parity and difference, then use a spreadsheet or chart like the one in Figure 8-2 to make a list of each.

Figure 8-2. **Your Differentiation Game Plan**

POINTS OF PARITY	POINTS OF DIFFERENCE
Qualities, skills, characteristics, experience, and education my competitors may offer	Qualities, skills, characteristics, experience, and education my competitors may not offer

Luke's Differentiation Game Plan might look like this:

> **Points of Parity:** I am enthusiastic, entrepreneurial, team-oriented, and good at solving problems. I communicate well with people. I understand the market for mental health care and what matters most to a startup business.

> **Points of Difference:** I am a trained physician with over ten years of experience in clinical care. My firsthand experience has taught me that my profession relies too heavily on prescription drugs dispensed by doctors with too little intimate knowledge of their patients' needs. My expanding education in entrepreneurship, combined with my clinical experience, gives me insight into how a technology-based system might deliver a higher standard of care.

If, like Luke and Joris, you have set your sights on landing a new position, then you will want to make sure you have taken a marketing approach to creating a convincing cover letter and attractive resume. Remember that people form first impressions in mere seconds. A 2012 study using eye-tracking technology found that recruiters looking at a resume make an initial fit/no-fit decision after only six seconds.[3] Put your unique educational accomplishments and their value in the workplace up front, where they will grab a reader's attention during that first glance. A word of caution: Even if you have taken twice as many business courses as someone with a conventional MBA, you cannot claim those initials on your resume. But you can make it crystal clear that you have put a tremendous amount of blood, sweat, and tears into getting the equivalent of an MBA, and that you have done it in order to provide great value to anyone who hires, promotes, or invests in you.

. 158 .

Figure 8-3

ASSEMBLE YOUR MARKETING FILE

. . . .

❒ **Showcase your self-directed business education** in your resume and cover letter. You will want to include clear, concise, and accurate descriptions of your accomplishments under the heading **Advanced Business Education (20XX–20XX)** or another similar heading. Consider using this basic template:

Advanced Business Education (20XX–20XX)

Online course work equivalent to a Master's in Business Administration, including Entrepreneurship (MIT Sloan), Corporate Finance (NYU Stern), Accounting (UPenn Wharton), and Business Strategy (UVA Darden), as well more than 15 other massive open online courses (MOOCs). Concentration in marketing. Portfolio at: www.nopaymba.com/yourname.

Caution: while recruiters generally view MOOCs and online learning as a positive accomplishment, listing a lot of introductory courses can make you look like a novice. While you certainly should take basic courses, make sure your resume highlights your advanced coursework and how it relates to the bigger picture of your nontraditional business education.

. . . .

❒ **Add bulleted highlights under at least one of your previous positions.** You want to show concrete examples of how your education helped you succeed in a position of responsibility. For example, under "Summer Internship at TechBox" you might bullet a specific accomplishment, such as "Used my knowledge of digital marketing to help the Marketing Director design a strategy for increasing online signups for extended service."

❐ **Tell your story in your cover letter.** You do not want to burden your reader with a lot of long-winded prose. Dedicate an early paragraph to your self-directed advanced business education, using a concrete example of how you've applied what you learned. It might go something like this:

After taking a series of courses on digital marketing from the University of Illinois (through the online platform Coursera), I ran A/B testing experiments to optimize the landing pages on TechBox's website. As a result, mailing list signups tripled, from 5% to 15% of visitors, and overall sales increased by 35%. My commitment to evidence-based decision making and the skills I learned while studying digital marketing will enable me to create, refine, and perfect any organization's online messages with measurable results.

❐ **Tweak your resume and cover letter to match each opportunity.** Think of each resume as a tailored glove made to fit an individual hand. If you are applying for work in the garment industry, highlight any interests and accomplishments that relate to that particular industry. Then, when you go for a position in the technology sector, adjust certain elements of your resume accordingly.

❐ **Keep it short and sweet.** You don't need to include everything you've ever done in a single, definitive library of achievements that goes to every prospective employer. Maintain a master resume that does include everything you've ever done, with bullets for every component of your job description and every accomplishment. Then, when you tweak it for a certain opportunity, you can easily pull what you need from that master document to create a tailored resume. The same applies to the cover letter.

❒ **Link, link, link.** Whenever you send a resume and cover letter electronically, provide live links to your portfolio, your website, and your relevant social media profiles (the professional ones, not the personal ones where you post pictures of your cat and your brother's wedding).

❒ **Seek help.** We've discussed the fact that MBA students in traditional programs work with career counselors to make sure they have written the best possible resumes and cover letters. You might want to invest a little money in a career coach or counselor.

Whole books have been written about the art of crafting strong resumes. I suggest you consult one of the better ones, Martin Yates's perennial bestseller *Knock 'Em Dead Resumes: A Killer Resume Gets More Job Interviews!*

Wow Them in Job Interviews

On a recent Tuesday, Ellen, the arts administrator you met in Chapter 4, logged into an online videoconference to interview for a position as the executive director of a symphony in a midsize American city. On her screen she saw ten interviewers sitting in one conference room, two in another location. One other person joined the group by phone. Uh-oh. Ellen imagined herself sweating through an intense grilling by thirteen people. As she struggled to calm the butterflies churning in her stomach, she tried her best to flash a warm smile, but in the back of her mind she was already preparing to move on to her second choice.

The interview began. One panelist asked Ellen about her current position in management at a small opera company. Another wondered about the strategic planning consulting she had done on the side for the Cincinnati Symphony Orchestra. As she fielded these questions, Ellen felt herself gradually loosening up. She loved her work and always exuded confidence when she talked about her passion for the business side of the arts.

Then one interviewer asked, "Why have you taken so many online business courses? Wouldn't you have been better off with a good old-fashioned MBA?" Since Ellen had listed her MOOC-based business studies in the Education section of her resume, she had expected some questions about her unconventional approach to business education. She explained her lifelong passion for music, as well as her realization that she couldn't build a stable career waiting for a role as a leading lady. Wishing to continue following her heart, she decided to look into the business side of the industry and quickly found that she enjoyed it as much as performing before a live audience. "I love learning, and MOOCs give me a chance to learn what I need when I need it, without costing me an arm and a leg." What turned her on about business? "I can help make an organization successful and profitable. That helps other musicians thrive." Why should anyone take a MOOC education seriously? "I got a top-notch education at some of the best business schools in the country. I also learned to seek value and to be financially savvy, an attitude I bring to management of arts organizations, which often have to stretch their limited resources. In fact, the accounting course I took from Wharton Business School has already helped with the budgeting process I'm leading in my current position." She could see her interviewers nodding their approval. Several scribbled notes as she talked.

Welcome to the most nerve-racking part of the job search: the live and in-person interview. However, you can put aside your fear when you realize you have reached a major milestone. To get your foot in the door, you must have done something right. Your marketing campaign is working. Now you just need to gather up your courage and leap over one final, albeit challenging, hurdle. Your compelling story will fuel that leap.

Before you sit down for an interview, face-to-face or online, make a list of the tough questions you expect to field. Then, look in the mirror and grill yourself. Rehearse your answers. As Ellen will tell you, performing well takes practice. As you perfect your answers, you may want to go back and make sure your credentials, your cover letter, and your resume reflect what you plan to say in response to the most difficult questions.

Interviewer: Why should we even consider someone who has only studied business online?

You: Because I have studied with the best professors from the best business schools (A and B and C Schools of Business), and because my successful track record proves my ability to put those lessons into practice.

Interviewer: Why does this position interest you?

You: Because I am passionate about this field (specific industry and function). My education will help me make a valuable contribution to your organization's (name) success.

Joris began his consulting career as a freelancer. During one of his assignments, he ran into an old classmate he hadn't seen in seven years. Imagine Joris's delight when he learned that his old friend could offer him a connection to a well-known consulting firm whose practice ran the gamut from management and IT consulting to education strategy. It sounded like a perfect fit. Through his friend, Joris arranged a meeting with one of the company's principals. After a wide-ranging and thought-provoking conversation, Joris hoped he might be offered a job on the spot. As if reading his mind, his interviewer said, "I really wish we had something open right now. Unfortunately, all of our positions are currently filled."

"That's okay," Joris said. "I think there could be an excellent fit here, and I would be happy to apply for a position as soon as there is one available." A few months later, Joris's patience paid off when the company called him back for another interview. Having thoroughly assembled his credentials and marketing file, he couldn't wait to field the toughest questions the interviewers might ask. Of course, he aced the interview, and he got the job.

POINTS TO REMEMBER

1. Treat your credentials not as pieces of paper but as elements of a strategy.
2. Validate your success with a mix of credentials, brand-name experience, personal recommendations, and impressive accomplishments.
3. Build your personal brand by demonstrating thought leadership, sharing your original ideas through blogging, presentations, or other media.
4. Think like a marketer when conducting your job search, particularly while preparing your resume, cover letter, and marketing file.
5. Highlight your self-directed business education in job interviews.

9

Learn Forever

Continuing Your Business
Education Throughout Your Career

MEET Karina, a lifelong learner we will follow as she moves from one self-directed learning opportunity to another throughout her career. A composite character drawn from my interactions with dozens of students over the years, she will illustrate the value of continuing your self-directed education long after you have reached your initial goals. After graduating from DePauw University with a degree in English literature, she relocated to Chicago, where she landed a job at the Perkins Public Relations Agency. Unlike many English majors, she actually put her education to work, writing press releases for the firm's clients. She loved the fast pace at PPR and found the work both challenging and engaging. But after a couple of years on the job, she grew bored with the daily routine and longed to move onto a career track that offered a greater opportunity for personal growth and financial success. While she enjoyed communicating other people's accomplishments, she wanted to get into the more creative side of the business. She knew in her heart that she could move beyond copywriting to a position where she could dream up the ideas behind the company's PR campaigns.

Karina set her sights on acquiring a solid business education without quitting her job, enrolled in a series of MOOCs that gave her the new skills she needed to climb the career ladder, and seized every opportunity to keep learning and growing throughout her life. MOOCs continued to figure prominently in her self-directed quest to acquire business skills and savvy, but she constantly looked for other opportunities to learn and grow. Like Karina, wherever you go and whatever you do in life, success will hinge on your ability to sharpen old skills and acquire new ones.

Keep Sharpening Your Skills

Whether you study beekeeping or branding strategy, your education will start to go out of date as soon as you finish your last course. That applies just as much to a MOOC education as any other form of learning. Fortunately, you can continually update a MOOC-based business education with a minimum investment of time and money. As a self-directed learner, you have not only learned a lot about business, you have mastered a *methodology* for learning that will benefit you throughout your life.

Using MOOCs and following the guidance in this book, Karina put herself through a rigorous business education with a concentration in brand strategy. She began her next career move by volunteering for a nonprofit health communications organization, where she could use her new business skills to assist with a total brand overhaul (including a slick new social media strategy). At the same time, she also formed relationships with a number of marketing professionals she met through the organization's network. These tactics enabled her to accomplish the shift from her PR job to a role with a small, fast-growing marketing firm, Brand Aid. Her writing skills, creativity, business savvy, and dedication to continuing her education made her an irresistible hire.

Even after landing a position with greater growth potential, Karina vowed to keep seeking ways to further develop her knowledge and skills. To that end, she found Class Central (https://class-central.com), the leading MOOC search engine, quite useful. If you sign up for automatic updates on your field of interest, you do not need to search every few months for learning opportunities. Class Central will automatically put them in your inbox. These updates helped Karina achieve her goal of completing one or two relevant MOOCs each year, either to explore new areas or to brush up any skills that had grown rusty.

For Karina, MOOCs have even come to her rescue at a few critical times in her career. When one of Brand Aid's larger clients sought to implement an "omni-channel" marketing strategy, Karina knew exactly where to go to learn about this cutting-edge marketing concept. In less than a week she was not only contributing valuable ideas to implement the client's strategy, she discovered a few risks no one else had detected. Becoming an "overnight expert" not only pleased the client, it impressed her boss so much that he put her in line to be the creative lead on new accounts the company acquired. "It's not that I try to outsmart everybody else," she says. "I just love to learn something *new*. It keeps me excited about my work."

That's a great word—*new*. The self-directed learners I meet invariably welcome change and seek out ways to harness it. The world of business keeps changing at such an accelerated rate, the preset curriculum at a stodgy business school cannot possibly keep up with it. During my own business studies, one startup company became an overnight billion-dollar sensation by radically changing the way people move from place to place. The new idea: Make it easy for people seeking rides to connect with drivers for hire. Voilà!

DON'T PAY FOR YOUR MBA

Uber quickly revolutionized a whole industry. It might take years for this phenomenon to become a case study in a typical business school curriculum, and a rigid set of course requirements might make it impossible to squeeze in an elective on the topic, even if one were offered. But in my own little business-school-of-one, I could be much more responsive. Toward the end of my studies, a course popped up that focused exclusively on Uber-style "platform businesses." Not only did *Platform Management, Strategy, and Innovation* explore the intricacies of this new business idea, it looked at how such businesses operate on the African continent, where I was living and working at the time. Taking the course exposed me to the *newest* ideas about the *newest* approach to business, all in the *newest* MBA program on earth, my own.

Win a Corporate Scholarship

One topic especially piqued Karina's interest during her studies: customer relationship management (CRM), the art and science of analyzing and strengthening interactions between an organization and its customers. Karina could see how CRM could play a crucial role in her own job as a branding strategist. Her coursework on digital marketing had stressed that the lines were blurring between these two marketing subtopics because a company's brand and its relationships with customers were inextricably intertwined. Yet, after a year at Brand Aid, Karina felt that the firm hadn't sufficiently linked the two. To make a case for doing that, she needed to learn a lot more about CRM, particularly the latest CRM software. A quick search of the MOOC platforms turned up nothing, but a little online research led her to a multi-week, online seminar class offered by a leading brand strategy firm. Unfortunately for the frugal Karina, it carried a hefty $2,000 price tag (not uncommon in the world of professional continuing education).

Sensing a win/win opportunity for both herself and Brand Aid, Karina approached her boss, Miles, with a proposition. "I really enjoy my work," she said, "and I am excited to continue to grow with Brand Aid. I've found a course that I think could really boost my skills and could open up some really exciting new avenues for the company."

Miles listened intently to her pitch. "I admire your initiative, Karina. You couldn't have brought this up at a better time. Coincidentally, I've been hearing a lot about CRM and was wondering how we could most easily and quickly look into the possibilities it might open up for us and our clients. Sign up tomorrow. We'll pick up the fee."

Never forget that your employer holds a major stake in your success. If you succeed, the company succeeds. Show your employer how your continuing business education can increase productivity and profitability and you may find yourself on the receiving end of a corporate "scholarship." Farsighted employers will eagerly invest in you, if they see how it will benefit the bottom line. Larger organizations often bring in consultants to train their people or send them to off-site training, all on the company's dime. If your company doesn't do that as a rule, show your initiative by suggesting it yourself, stressing the potential cost savings and revenue increase by saying something like, "This training program could teach us ways to save on costs and increase our revenues."

Continuous learning makes you more and more valuable to employers. As Randall Stephenson, CEO of AT&T, told the *New*

York Times in 2016, "There is a need to retool yourself, and you should not expect to stop." Stephenson suggested that a five- to ten-hour investment per week in online learning can keep you from becoming obsolete.[1] Acquiring more and more knowledge not only keeps you up-to-date, it also helps you get ahead where you currently work or land a better job down the street.

In Karina's case, after convincing Miles to sponsor her first course on CRM, she independently dove deep into the topic, learning about a variety of software solutions and reading John Goodman's *Customer Experience 3.0*. Her final report to Miles suggested that Brand Aid form a separate unit to focus on CRM. "Great idea, Karina," he said. "I'd like you to head it up."

Tap Your Network

Karina stood at a whiteboard, furiously jotting down ideas as the group proposed them. "We could organize a walk-to-work day for the city," a Brand Aid CRM teammate suggested.

A manager from Chicago's Recreation Department raised her hand. "How about a month-long competition with teams logging miles on pedometers?"

"We might hold a Biggest Loser competition with local celebrities," called out the director of Corporate Social Responsibility (CSR) for a Chicago-based telecommunications company.

The CRM team had invited local officials and prominent businesspeople to join them in brainstorming ways to promote an exercise program sponsored by Clearly Health, a new Brand Aid client. The group was applying what they had learned after taking an online course in human-centered design.

When Karina had first suggested that her team and a half-dozen city officials and business leaders take an online course together, she worried that they might balk at the idea. Few had even flirted with online education. She fretted needlessly, however, because her team had seen the results of Karina's own self-directed business education. Clearly Health signed on enthusiastically. Even the city health director was excited about the initiative, which supported a citywide wellness campaign he championed. Everyone enjoyed the course Karina had selected: *Design Kit: The Course for Human-Centered Design*. The group of ten met at Clearly Health's office in downtown Chicago one evening a week during the run of the course. Karina loved the way everyone had gotten excited about designing a program that would to inspire citizens to tie on their walking shoes and get moving.

In Chapter 6, we explored ways to grow your network by finding or forming a learning group, as Arjan did when he reached out to the startup community in his city. You can keep benefiting from your own "network university" long after you've finished the main portion of your studies. You might continue to nurture the learning group you found or formed earlier in your studies, checking in periodically or even taking a course together from time to time. You might also consider forming a group at your place of work or pulling together people from both inside and outside your organization who share common interests. Even if you don't think you can afford the time and energy to organize a group course, consider inviting a professional acquaintance, someone with whom you wish to forge a stronger relationship, to take a course with you. Studying together, like walking together, can keep you moving forward while you develop a stronger professional and personal relationship.

Try convincing your employer to sponsor learning initiatives for employees. More and more corporate executives appreciate the value-adding power of continuing education. If you are a millennial like Karina, you probably feel comfortable with online learning already. If you are a seasoned manager like her boss, Miles, it may take a course or two before you see the benefits.

Bruce, another lifelong learner in my network, could have retired years ago, but he could not see himself sitting on his front porch watching the sun rise and set. Instead, he spends his days working with executives to create learning cultures in the workplace. The "learning circles" he creates foster employee development and stronger work relationships. In the old days, he relied on books such as Peter Drucker's *The Effective Executive* to spark discussions and impart new knowledge and skills. To maximize results through a company, the circles included both senior and junior employees from various departments. Over the years, Bruce's learning circles have come to incorporate a variety of tools, including not just books but also videos and online games. Then along came MOOCs. While the format of the circles did not change, MOOCs added a powerful new tool to the experience. *Learning How to Learn*, the popular MOOC that applies to any learning endeavor, generated an amazing response. People loved this approach to learning and sharing ideas. Several C-suite executives became big fans. As Bruce told me, "They would say things like, 'Nobody ever taught me how to learn. I'm going to suggest that everyone at my company take this course.'" Consider serving as a catalyst for a learning culture in your own workplace. It's a great way to acquire and sharpen important skills. Internal, external, two people or ten, networks built for learning can help create a competitive edge for any organization.

Go Global

In recent years global business has become an increasingly popular topic in MBA programs, MOOC courses, and online concentrations. Regardless of your own area of interest, you will find that it crosses international borders. Many traditional MBA programs stress this fact and encourage global travel. Some even incorporate the cost into their regular fee structure. That can add a big chunk of change to the cost of acquiring an MBA. As the director of your own personal MBA program, you can find creative ways to gain some international experience by combining travel with learning. Even without a budget for major trips to exotic places, you can explore many different ways to expand your horizons beyond your home country.

First, taking courses that are produced in other countries offers one easy and affordable way to dip your toe into the global pool. You don't necessarily need to know Chinese to take a course from Tsinghua University because, like movies that come from overseas, many programs offer subtitles and the option to fulfill assignments in your native tongue. By taking a course produced in a foreign culture, you not only learn content you want to master, you also pick up information about how business operates in that culture. For example, when I studied accounting, I took two courses, one produced in the United States and one produced in Australia. I knew that the two countries employed different accounting systems: the Generally Accepted Accounting Principles in the States, and the International Financial Reporting Standards down under. My MOOC coursework allowed me to "travel" to Australia and learn from a professor with experience in a system other than the one most commonly used in my home country.

Second, you will often find people from many different countries taking a particular course. Some of the courses I've highlighted in this book, such as *Beyond Silicon Valley* and *Successful Negotiation*, explicitly address cultural differences in business techniques. Professor George Siedel encourages students to partner with someone from a different country during *Successful Negotiation*'s final exercise. You may have an entirely different experience when you partner with a Dutch student versus a Russian, Japanese, or Canadian classmate. Even if a course you are taking doesn't address international differences, you can and should extend a welcoming hand to classmates from different regions of the world. You can even form an international study group, complete with global videoconferences. You will find such virtual international "travel" both informative and enriching.

Many self-directed learners from around the world have also discovered that MOOCs offer an excellent way to refine their business vocabulary in a second language. Many foreign-based MOOC students report that studying in English gives them a double boost: a new vocabulary and deeper insight into the way Americans conduct business. Li, a Chinese student, says, "I mainly take courses in English because during the learning process, my English ability can be improved as well. For Chinese students interested in studying business, I think they—including me—need to be more open-minded about trying new ways of studying, and not be afraid of English-only lessons." If you are planning to study business in a second language (as opposed to business *as* a second language, which we covered in Chapter 3), I suggest starting with a basic course where you already know a good deal of the subject matter. Then you can gradually work your way up to more difficult or unfamiliar subjects. In my own case, taking a MOOC on credit risk analysis in French left me with tremendous respect for students who take all of their coursework in a second language. I watched the entire first video wondering what the professor meant by the word *actions*. Finally, it dawned on me (after consulting a glossary of French business terms) that "action" meant "share." The same happened with the word *bénéfice*, which translates not as "benefit" but as "earnings." Unfortunately, by the time I had figured out that "benefit per action" was actually "earnings per share," I needed to go back and watch the entire lecture again. Even if you struggle with a language, take heart. You will, in the end, pick up valuable vocabulary and cultural information even if you don't decipher every single word.

Third, you can get a lot out of courses designed for entrepreneurs in the developing world. Courses such as *Global Social Entrepreneurship* (Philanthropy U via NovoEd), *Innovation and Design for Global Grand Challenges* (Duke University via Coursera), and *Subsistence Marketplaces* (University of Illinois at Urbana-Champaign via Coursera) focus on business solutions to the problem of global poverty, often attracting a large number of students from outside of the United States and Europe. You can use these courses to expand your horizons, grow your international network, and train yourself to use business tools for social impact. However you go about it, acquiring knowledge of the global arena can benefit you in many ways. You may end up working with a U.S. company based in Korea or for a Korean company with offices in the United States. In either case, you will learn new ways of conducting business, teach foreign colleagues new words and techniques, and make a lot of friends along the way.

Karina got some unexpected global experience when Brand Aid took on a Peruvian client, Estilo Central, which was looking to expand into the North American market by opening a flagship clothing and apparel store in Chicago. She knew she needed to understand a lot more about Peruvian culture and customs before she designed a marketing campaign for the company. Miles agreed that she should travel to Lima where she could get to know the people who worked for Estilo Central and immerse herself in the local culture. She spent a few weeks brushing up on her high school Spanish (with the help of a MOOC or two). Imagine her surprise when she found the executives at Estilo Central speaking fluent English. Still, her basic vocabulary came in handy, and it did not take long for her to pick up some Peruvian expressions and develop an appreciation for the bright colors and fine fabrics the local women preferred.

Once she had wrapped up the business side of her trip, she spent a week of vacation time exploring Lima and the surrounding countryside, even taking a day trip to an alpaca farm where Estilo Central sourced wool for its unique sweaters. She was so happy to find the perfect guide in Gustavo, a classmate from one of her entrepreneurship courses. He taught her more about Peruvian culture and entrepreneurship than she could have gotten from the best business school in the world.

Live and Learn

MOOCs are for business, but MOOCS are for life as well. Now that you know your way around the world of self-directed education, you can broaden your perspective to learn anything and everything you need to know to succeed in life as well as business. You might study a subject, such as jewelry-making or basket-weaving, just for the fun of it, or you might take a course that sends you on a whole new career trajectory, as Karina did.

At age 55, married and with her two daughters off to college, Karina decided to follow a dream that had begun to form when she was pregnant with her twins: maternal and child health. After taking two courses on the subject, *Midwifery* (Open2Study) and *Childbirth: A Global Perspective* (Coursera), she decided to retire from Brand Aid and embark on a new career in public health communication. She started her new career with a consultancy through the World Health Organization, where she could use her years of experience with branding and marketing to create communications materials to reach pregnant and nursing women in sub-Saharan Africa. Whether you do it for fun or profit, you can keep feeding your hunger for new knowledge and skills by creating and occasionally updating a Lifelong Learning Plan (see Figure 9-1).

Figure 9-1

▶ ADVISER'S CHALLENGE ◀

CREATE YOUR LONG-TERM LEARNING PLAN

☐ **Visualize yourself in five, ten, and fifteen years.** Where do you see yourself at each of these milestones, personally and professionally? What might you need to learn along the way? Jot down a few notes about each stage, connecting your goals with specific courses and areas of expertise. Like Karina, you may make a major shift later in life.

☐ **Learn something just for the fun of it.** If you've been immersing yourself in business subjects, you might want to take a "learning vacation," studying something that you've always wanted to do.

- ❏ **Make learning a habit.** If you've finished the intensive part of your business education, you should not put your learning plan on hold. Try to learn something new every year. Every January 1, Karina adds one course for her career and one for fun to her New Year's resolutions.

- ❏ **Identify areas for further growth.** You know your strengths and weaknesses. You can select a course to build on a strength or shore up a weakness. Karina kept taking courses that sharpened her already impressive writing skills, but she also took math-oriented courses than helped conquer her uneasiness with numbers.

- ❏ **Consult the learning advocates in your life.** Certain friends, colleagues, and family members have encouraged your self-directed education. Periodically ask these learning advocates for input on where your learning journey might take you next.

- ❏ **Track your continuing education.** You might use a spreadsheet or a paper journal to keep a written record of your educational journey. Or let Degreed.com do it for you. Degreed pulls data from all the MOOC platforms and can also track articles and books you read, videos you watch, and pretty much any other kind of media you might consume. It can also help you identify courses, books, and articles related to new fields of study that strike your fancy.

Watch for the Next Big Thing

If you are like most MOOC enthusiasts, you are an independent, self-directed, entrepreneurial sort of person. You may have launched a career in a field with a long history in the business world, such as accounting and finance or marketing and sales in the automotive industry; or you may have plunged into one of the cutting-edge industries that did not even exist before the dawn of the MOOC, such as management and leadership in the world of artificial intelligence. Wherever you find yourself at any given moment in your career, keep your eyes open for the Next Big Thing. In 2015, the career website PayScale listed five high-paying careers that didn't even exist ten years ago, including Data Scientist, Mobile Applications Developer, Information Security Analyst, and Digital Strategist.[2] You might become a pioneer in one of those jobs or in one not yet invented. You might one day start a business in a field that doesn't yet exist. Even if you stay in the same role in the same industry throughout your career, you can reap huge benefits from bringing the Next Big Thing into your workplace. Karina did all three: She became a widely respected authority on the latest CRM software, she brought it into the Brand Aid office, and she started a side business offering CRM consulting to not-for-profit charities.

The business world changes at light speed. So does the universe of online learning. Anant Agarwal, CEO of the MOOC platform edX, has often emphasized that edX exists not only to increase access to education but also to study how people learn online, thereby generating insight that can improve both in-person and digital teaching. A 2014 study tracked 100,000 edX learners and found that students would most likely succeed in courses featuring short videos (less than six minutes) with fast-talking professors and lots of engaging visuals.[3] As these sorts of studies generate more insight, course delivery will likely change to reflect the growing body of evidence about how people learn.

Other platforms, such as Coursera, have also experimented with ways to enhance learning. Last year, Coursera piloted project-based courses, emphasizing real-world problems, and mentor-based courses, which include one-on-one feedback and live office hours with industry professionals. Karina's college-age kids will follow their mother into the world of self-directed learning, but the MOOCs they take will not be the prehistoric ones their mother took.

Next Big Things will also alter the MOOC landscape, driven not just by the course platforms but also by the startups that have sprung up in their wake. MOOCLab.club and Mentive offer opportunities for sharing materials and joining facilitated learning communities. Degreed has set its sights on "jailbreaking the degree." Its manifesto proclaims, "The challenges of the future won't care how you became an expert, just that you did."[4] Degreed offers wonderful tools for lifelong learners, including ways for you to find new learning opportunities, track your progress, and measure your success.

Credentialing will also evolve. Udacity premiered Nanodegrees, edX introduced MicroMasters, Coursera partnered with the University of Illinois to offer the iMBA, and FutureLearn teamed up with Australia's Deakin University to offer a suite of postgraduate degrees. Expect more and more offerings that make self-directed learning widely accepted and respected in the business world. Karina, our poster child for lifelong learning, followed all of these developments with keen interest. And she made sure she passed them along to her daughters.

Pay It Forward

Pay It Forward, a 2000 film about a young boy who launches a goodwill movement, shows how we can all make the world a better place by passing along kindness, favors, and good deeds.

Rather than "paying it back" to the person who helped us out, we can "pay it forward" to someone else in need. The film and the concept it advocates offer a wonderful lesson for self-directed learners. You embarked on your journey toward a virtual MBA in order to improve yourself and your chances of succeeding in your business career. You can stop there, or you can pay it forward.

In 2016, the total number of people who registered for at least one MOOC grew to 58 million. Twenty-three million of those were first-time MOOC users.[5] How many more people around the world could benefit from knowing that MOOCs exist? You can play a role in getting the word out by sharing your experience with other potential self-directed learners. Some MOOCs encourage students who have excelled in a course to serve as mentors for others. Hillary, the single mom and entrepreneur who appeared in Chapter 1 and again in Chapter 6, has served as a Course Catalyst mentor for several +Acumen courses on NovoEd. Look for similar opportunities during your coursework. You can also share your experience through writing, teaching, and advising, both online and in-person. All of the techniques we've discussed in previous chapters, from discovering where you can best contribute to growing your network, sharing your ideas, and building your personal brand, can help you inform and inspire the next generation of learners. Do any local organizations provide support to entrepreneurs, help young people learn about business, or match students with mentors? If so, join one; if not, start one. If you haven't taught before, you may find you have a knack for imparting knowledge to others. Most self-directed learners do. As a teacher, you will likely find that you learn and benefit from the experience just as much as your students do.

As for Karina, while still employed at Brand Aid, she started her own consulting firm on the side, teaching CRM techniques to not-for-profit charities. Everywhere she went, both as a Brand Aid manager and as an independent consultant, she not only promoted this powerful software, she also championed the MOOC experience that made her an expert in the field. After cultivating contacts in the media, she arranged for a number of interviews with reporters from such major outlets as *Forbes* and the *Huffington Post*, who spread her story far and wide. In addition to writing and consulting, she also spent a semester teaching at night as an adjunct professor in the business department of a local junior college. If she could afford the time, she would do a lot more public speaking, but she has found it necessary to pick and choose her sharing opportunities. "If only there were twelve days in a week, I could double my influence. I think *everybody* should be empowered to continue learning!" Of course, after she moved on from Brand Aid and plunged headlong into the business of international development, she kept putting her communication skills to work both on the job and as an advocate for self-directed learning.

POINTS TO REMEMBER

1. Keep up the learning habit by continuing to take online courses as the need arises and to remain at the cutting edge of your field.
2. Learn and grow at work by taking advantage of employer-sponsored training opportunities and by identifying courses that can enhance your work.
3. Continue to nurture your network, using MOOCs as the basis for building professional relationships.
4. Take your MOOC education overseas, virtually or in-person.

5. Be on the lookout for and open to taking advantage of innovations in the world of MOOCs and online learning.
6. Share your skills and knowledge with future online learners, and inspire them to take control of their own continuing education and career development.

CONCLUSION

Believe in Yourself

I would like to close with a confession. Before I finally took the initiative to study business on my own, I spent years feeling insecure and out of place in the world of work. When I graduated from college, I mistakenly thought I would land a great job with the snap of my fingers. After all, I had proved myself as a reliable worker, having held jobs in a bookstore during high school, at an arts camp and a national park during summer vacations from college, and even during the school year in the campus career center. But when I went looking for that dream job, I found myself swimming in a vast sea of degree-holding job seekers, all vying for a limited number of entry-level positions. After the first few rejections, I began to question myself. Why did I keep falling short? Submitting yet more resumes and cover letters took all my courage, as I began to expect that dreaded, "Thank you for applying, but. . . ."

Even when I managed to clear the almost insurmountable hurdle of *getting* a job, I worried myself sick about actually *doing* the job. Early on I won a position as a sustainable business development consultant at the International Finance Corporation, part of the World Bank Group. I liked my fancy title, and I enjoyed the work, but every time I heard my coworkers talking about return on investment, due diligence, or CAPEX, I felt like an imposter. I often thought about getting an MBA, which seemed like the only antidote to those feelings of insecurity. Once I could print those three letters behind my name, I assumed I would sail through the hiring process, waltz into any job interview brimming with confidence, wow the interviewers, accept a terrific job offer, and go to work each day with a sense of security and satisfaction, knowing that I truly belonged in the workplace. However, as I pondered the reality of investing a huge chunk of time and money in a traditional MBA program, I could not stomach the prospect of graduating with that coveted degree, only to be buried under a mountain of debt.

When I began to study business on my own as a MOOC neophyte, I quickly saw a way through my MBA dilemma. At the time, I was working as a rural enterprise and entrepreneurship specialist for the U.S. Agency for International Development in Rwanda. Again, I secretly worried that I really didn't know enough about either enterprises or entrepreneurship to deserve my title. Through my courses, I gathered the knowledge and skills I needed. I studied the relevant topics both in general business courses and in ones tailored to emerging economies, courses such as *Beyond Silicon Valley: Growing Entrepreneurship in Transitioning Economies* and *Subsistence Marketplaces*. Almost overnight, I became comfortable discussing price-risk hedging in agricultural markets, consumer demand, and firm-level investment. The more courses I took and the more skills I gained, the more confident I felt, and the more value I contributed to my team. No longer did I feel like an imposter. I had turned myself into the real thing, a fully prepared professional who deserved her place in the business world.

Later I learned that so many people share my workplace anxiety that the condition has its own name: Imposter Syndrome. A

2014 article in *The Atlantic* explored just how common such a lack of confidence is among women and how greatly it hinders their future growth.[1] And while women may particularly fall prey to feeling like imposters, so do young people, people of color, and anyone who sets big goals, takes large risks, and strives to keep advancing in their career. Fortunately, there is a sure cure for Imposter Syndrome: education, knowledge, and skills. Even more fortunately, that cure is now more readily available and affordable than ever before.

Two years after I started my business education, my employer sent me from Rwanda to Washington, D.C., to attend a short training course on global financial markets. The course, designed to teach foreign aid professionals to explore collaboration and partnership with bankers, investors, and fund managers, was taught by a fast-talking former New York finance professional who filled a whiteboard with cost curves, waxing poetic about the structure of financial deals and going into great detail about the risks of conducting financial transactions in foreign markets. I found the course an enjoyable review of the material I had studied in my classes. During a break, I was standing beside another woman attending the course who was pouring herself a cup of coffee. "I must say, I'm feeling pretty lost in this course," she confessed. "You ask such good questions. I can tell you really know this stuff. Where did you get your MBA?"

I couldn't help but smile. "Actually, I *don't* have an MBA," I said. "But I have studied business. If you're interested, I can show you how I did it."

From experience, I know that your self-directed business education can help you reach your goals. The same year I attended that course on global financial markets, I was promoted into a position usually reserved for someone with a classical MBA. And I'm not the only one. Remember Mark, the engineer you met in Chapter 7? He will soon become the first-ever "people analytics manager" at his company. His employer actually created this position especially for him when it became clear how much value his specialized online education and passion could bring to the company. He recently updated me on his career progress: "I just wanted to let you know how effective MOOCs and your methods were in helping me make a pivot in my career."

Of course, I wish you great success in your career, but even more, I hope you will gain the sense of empowerment, confidence, and accomplishment that Mark and I have felt as our nontraditional business educations have garnered us such great personal and professional rewards. As you know from reading this book, I collect stories about people who have done what Mark and I have done. I'd love to hear yours. You can share it in the No-Pay MBA Facebook group, send it through the contact form at NoPayMBA.com, or address it directly to me at: laurie@nopaymba.com. I'll be waiting to hear from you.

ACKNOWLEDGMENTS

My thanks go to Stephen S. Power, who first suggested I write a book based on my experiences, and to Executive Editor Ellen Kadin at AMACOM, who swooped in to take it across the finish line. I owe a special debt of gratitude to Michael and Patricia Snell, for their belief in the potential of this book (and in my potential as an author) and for patiently guiding me into the world of book publishing. During the process of writing and editing the book, Michael served as a phenomenal writing partner, coach, teacher, and spirit guide.

Thanks also to all the members of the No-Pay MBA Network, especially those who helped me build and shape it, including Nick Switzer, Kristof Neirinck, Hillary Strobel, Brandi Johnson, Louisa Shepherd, Andrew Martz, and Arjan Tupan. Nick Switzer deserves special recognition for reaching out early on to share his inspiring story of self-directed learning. I deeply appreciate the contributions of all the other learners who have shared their stories with me in interviews, emails, social media posts, and comments on the blog. It really does take a community to create a book.

My parents, Bob and Cathy Pickard, have always championed my thirst for learning. I can never find the words to tell them how much their support has always meant to me. My deepest thanks

ACKNOWLEDGMENTS

also go to my husband, Daniel Handel. His support and encouragement made this entire project possible. Finally, I must offer thanks to the two new additions to our family, Holly and Owen, for staying in their increasingly cramped quarters long enough for me to finish writing this book.

APPENDIX A

Recommended Courses by Subject

This list, by no means complete, includes representative courses available on the major MOOC platforms. I can personally recommend many of these courses, which I or other students have taken. This list also includes input from Dhawal Shah, founder of the top MOOC search engine Class Central. You might consider choosing courses from this list. You might also find it quite useful to rely on Class-Central.com to lead you to the most up-to-date and comprehensive listing of open courses.

Big-Picture Thinking Courses

DESIGN THINKING

Design Kit: The Course for Human-Centered Design • IDEO.org, +Acumen (NovoEd)

Design Thinking for Innovation • Professor Jeanne Liedtka, University of Virginia Darden School of Business (Coursera)

ENTREPRENEURSHIP

Beyond Silicon Valley • Professor Michael Goldberg, Case Western Reserve University Weatherhead School of Management (Coursera)

Entrepreneurship 101: What Is Your Product? • Professor Bill Aulet and Lecturer Erdin Beshamov, MITx (edX)

Entrepreneurship 102: Do You Have a Product? • Professor Bill Aulet and Lecturer Erdin Beshamov, MITx (edX)

Get Your Startup Started • One of five free technology entrepreneurship courses from Google (Udacity)

How to Build a Startup • Steve Blank (Udacity)

ETHICS AND DECISION MAKING

New Models of Business in Society • Professor R. Freeman, University of Virginia Darden School of Business (Coursera)

The Three-Pillar Model for Business Decisions: Strategy, Law, and Ethics • Professor George Siedel, University of Michigan (Coursera)

MARKETING

Digital Branding and Engagement • Professor Sonia Dickinson, Curtin University (edX)

Introduction to Marketing • Professors Barbara E. Kahn, Peter Fader, and David Bell, University of Pennsylvania Wharton School of Business (Coursera)

Introduction to Marketing • Professors Darren Dahl and Paul Cubbon, The University of British Columbia (edX)

Marketing in a Digital World • Professor Aric Rindfleisch, University of Illinois at Urbana-Champaign (Coursera)

STRATEGY

Competitive Strategy and Organization Design Specialization (4 courses) • Ludwig-Maximilians-Universität München (Coursera)

Foundations of Business Strategy • Professor Michael Lenox, University of Virginia Darden School of Business (Coursera)

General Business and Personal Development Courses

An Entire MBA in 1 Course • Professor Chris Haroun (Udemy)

Learning How to Learn: Powerful Mental Tools to Help You Master Tough Subjects • Professors Barbara Oakley and Terry Sejnowski, University of California San Diego (Coursera)

Successful Negotiation: Essential Skills and Strategies • Professor George Siedel, University of Michigan (Coursera)

The Science of Success: What Researchers Know That You Should Know • Professor Paula Caproni, University of Michigan (Coursera)

Working in Teams: A Practical Guide • Professors Lydia Kavanagh and David Neil, University of Queensland (edX)

Management and Leadership Courses

COMMUNICATION

Communicating Strategically • Professors Bart Collins and Melanie Morgan, Purdue University (edX)

Intercultural Communication • Steve Kulich, Honling Zhang, and Ruobing Chi, Shanghai International Studies University (FutureLearn)

MANAGING PEOPLE

Managing Talent • Professors Scott DeRue, Maxim Sytch, and Cheri Alexander, University of Michigan Ross School of Business (Coursera)

People Management • Professor Vasanthi Srinivasan, Indian Institute of Management Bangalore (edX)

LEADERSHIP

Inspired Leadership Specialization (5 courses) • Case Western Reserve University (Coursera)

Leadership Communication for Maximum Impact: Storytelling • Professor Tom Collinger, Northwestern University (Coursera)

Management and Leadership: Growing as a Manager • Angela Lilley, The Open University (FutureLearn)

Organizational Leadership Specialization (6 courses) • Northwestern University (Coursera)

Strategic Leadership and Management Specialization (7 courses) • University of Illinois (Coursera)

OPERATIONS MANAGEMENT

Introduction to Operations Management • Professor Christian Terwiesch, University of Pennsylvania Wharton School of Business (Coursera)

PROJECT MANAGEMENT

Fundamentals of Project Planning and Management • Professor Yael Grushka-Cockayne, University of Virginia Darden School of Business (Coursera)

Introduction to Project Management • Various instructors, The University of Adelaide (edX)

OTHER MANAGEMENT TOPICS

Critical Perspectives on Management • Professor Rolf Strom-Olsen, IE Business School (Coursera)

Managing the Organization: From Organizational Design to Execution • Professor Huseyin Leblebici, University of Illinois (Coursera)

Quantitative and Financial Analysis Courses

ACCOUNTING

Introduction to Financial Accounting • Professor Brian Bushee, University of Pennsylvania Wharton School of Business (Coursera)

DATA ANALYSIS

Business Analytics Specialization (5 courses) • University of Pennsylvania Wharton School of Business (Coursera)

Data Analysis and Presentation Skills: The PwC Approach Specialization (5 courses) • PricewaterhouseCoopers (Coursera)

Data Science Specialization (10 courses) • Johns Hopkins University (Coursera)

FINANCE

Corporate Finance • Professor Aswath Damodaran, New York University Stern School of Business (iTunes U)

Financial Markets • Professor Robert Shiller, Yale University (Coursera)

Financial Modeling for the Social Sector • Professor Erik Simanis, PhilanthropyU (NovoEd)

Introduction to Corporate Finance • Professor Michael R. Roberts, University of Pennsylvania Wharton School of Business (Coursera)

Introduction to Finance: Valuation and Investing Specialization (5 courses) • University of Michigan Ross School of Business (Coursera)

Intro to Financial Modeling • Symon He and Brandon Young (Udemy)

APPENDIX B

Sample Study Plans

These charts illustrate two typical approaches to structuring your studies. Always keep in mind, however, that every student brings a unique set of experiences, needs, and goals to the task of acquiring a business education. Your particular plan will depend on a number of factors, including the amount of time you can devote to your studies each week, your specific career goals, and the subjects that you find most interesting and useful. The first chart shows a nine-month, accelerated study plan for students who plan to dedicate twenty hours per week to their studies. The second plan demonstrates how students who can devote ten hours per week to their studies might structure an eighteen-month course of study to reach their business education goals.

9-Month Plan

	ACADEMICS	OUTSIDE THE CLASSROOM
Months 1–3	Core Curriculum (Chapter 3)	Explore career options (Chapter 5) Find/form a learning community (Chapter 6) Build and expand network (Chapter 6)
Months 4–6	Essential Business Skills (Chapter 4)	Select an MBA concentration (Chapter 7) Continue to expand network, conduct informational interviews (Chapter 6)
Months 7–9	MBA Concentration Coursework and Culmination Project (Chapter 7)	Prepare digital portfolio, resume, and other marketing materials for job search (Chapters 7–8)

18-Month Plan

	ACADEMICS	OUTSIDE THE CLASSROOM
Months 1–3	Core Curriculum (Chapter 3)	
Months 4–6	Core Curriculum (Chapter 3)	Find/form a learning community (Chapter 6)
Months 7–9	Essential Business Skills (Chapter 4)	Explore career options (Chapter 5) Select an MBA concentration (Chapter 7)
Months 10–12	Essential Business Skills (Chapter 4)	Build and expand network, conduct informational interviews (Chapter 6)
Months 13–15	MBA Concentration Course-work (Chapter 7)	Continue to build and expand network (Chapter 6) Build online, shareable portfolio (Chapter 7)
Months 16–18	MBA Culmination Project (Chapter 7)	Prepare resume and other job search marketing materials (Chapter 8)

APPENDIX C

Sample Course Lists for Various MBA Concentrations

These sample course lists reflect possible course progressions for several MBA concentrations. The world of MOOCs evolves rapidly, so the array of subjects and specific courses may have expanded a lot since this book was published. Your individual course plan will vary depending on the concentration you choose, the electives that interest you, and the courses that are available when you design your program.

Sample Course List 1, Concentration: Finance

FOUNDATION COURSES

❏ **Self-directed learning**
Learning How to Learn: Powerful Mental Tools to Help You Master Tough Subjects • Professors Barbara Oakley and Terry Sejnowski, University of California San Diego (Coursera)

❏ **Finance**
Introduction to Corporate Finance • Professor Michael R. Roberts, University of Pennsylvania Wharton School of Business (Coursera)

❏ **Accounting**
Introduction to Financial Accounting • Professor Brian Bushee, University of Pennsylvania Wharton School of Business (Coursera)

❏ **General business**
An Entire MBA in 1 Course • Professor Chris Haroun (Udemy)

❏ **Marketing**
Introduction to Marketing • Professors Barbara E. Kahn, Peter Fader, and David Bell, University of Pennsylvania Wharton School of Business (Coursera)

SKILL-BUILDING AND ELECTIVE COURSES

❏ **Financial modeling**
Intro to Financial Modeling • Symon He and Brandon Young (Udemy)

❏ **Data analysis**
Data Analysis and Presentation Skills: The PwC Approach Specialization (5 courses) • PricewaterhouseCoopers (Coursera)

❏ **Negotiation**
Successful Negotiation: Essential Skills and Strategies • Professor George Siedel, University of Michigan (Coursera)

❏ **Entrepreneurship**
How to Build a Startup • Steve Blank (Udacity)

❏ **Business strategy**
Foundations of Business Strategy • Professor Michael Lenox, University of Virginia Darden School of Business (Coursera)

❏ **Business ethics**
New Models of Business in Society • Professor R. Freeman, University of Virginia Darden School of Business (Coursera)

CONCENTRATION COURSES

❏ **Corporate finance**
Corporate Finance • Professor Aswath Damodaran, New York University Stern School of Business (iTunes U)

❏ **Investing, markets**
Financial Markets • Professor Robert Shiller, Yale University (Coursera)

❏ **Financial modeling**
Financial Modeling for the Social Sector • Professor Erik Simanis, PhilanthropyU (NovoEd)

❏ **Financial valuation**
Introduction to Finance: Valuation and Investing Specialization (5 courses) • University of Michigan Ross School of Business (Coursera)

Sample Course List 2, Concentration: Entrepreneurship

FOUNDATION COURSES

☐ **Self-directed learning**
Learning How to Learn: Powerful Mental Tools to Help You Master Tough Subjects • Professors Barbara Oakley and Terry Sejnowski, University of California San Diego (Coursera)

☐ **General business**
An Entire MBA in 1 Course • Professor Chris Haroun (Udemy)

☐ **Entrepreneurship**
How to Build a Startup • Steve Blank (Udacity)

☐ **Marketing**
Introduction to Marketing • Professors Barbara E. Kahn, Peter Fader, and David Bell, University of Pennsylvania Wharton School of Business (Coursera)

☐ **Business ethics**
The Three-Pillar Model for Business Decisions: Strategy, Law, and Ethics • Professor George Siedel, University of Michigan (Coursera)

SKILL-BUILDING AND ELECTIVE COURSES

☐ **Design thinking**
Design Thinking for Innovation • Professor Jeanne Liedtka, University of Virginia Darden School of Business (Coursera)

☐ **Branding**
Digital Branding and Engagement • Professor Sonia Dickinson, Curtin University (edX)

☐ **Leadership**
Inspired Leadership Specialization (5 courses) • Case Western Reserve University (Coursera)

☐ **Project management**
Introduction to Project Management • Various instructors, The University of Adelaide (edX)

☐ **Financial modeling**

Intro to Financial Modeling • Symon He and Brandon Young (Udemy)

☐ **Negotiation**

Successful Negotiation: Essential Skills and Strategies • Professor George Siedel, University of Michigan (Coursera)

☐ **Business strategy**

Foundations of Business Strategy • Professor Michael Lenox, University of Virginia Darden School of Business (Coursera)

CONCENTRATION COURSES

☐ **Entrepreneurship**

Beyond Silicon Valley • Professor Michael Goldberg, Case Western Reserve University Weatherhead School of Management (Coursera)

Entrepreneurship 101: What Is Your Product? • Professor Bill Aulet and Lecturer Erdin Beshamov, MITx (edX)

Entrepreneurship 102: Do You Have a Product? • Professor Bill Aulet and Lecturer Erdin Beshamov, MITx (edX)

Entrepreneurship: Launching an Innovative Business Specialization (4 courses) • University of Maryland (Coursera)

Sample Course List 3, Concentration: Marketing

FOUNDATION COURSES

☐ **Self-directed learning**

Learning How to Learn: Powerful Mental Tools to Help You Master Tough Subjects • Professors Barbara Oakley and Terry Sejnowski, University of California San Diego (Coursera)

☐ **Marketing**

Introduction to Marketing • Professors Barbara E. Kahn, Peter Fader, and David Bell, University of Pennsylvania Wharton School of Business (Coursera)

☐ Finance
Introduction to Corporate Finance • Professor Michael R. Roberts, University of Pennsylvania Wharton School of Business (Coursera)

☐ Entrepreneurship
How to Build a Startup • Steve Blank (Udacity)

SKILL-BUILDING AND ELECTIVE COURSES

☐ Project management
Introduction to Project Management • Various instructors, The University of Adelaide (edX)

☐ Design thinking
Design Thinking for Innovation • Professor Jeanne Liedtka, University of Virginia Darden School of Business (Coursera)

☐ Business strategy
Foundations of Business Strategy • Professor Michael Lenox, University of Virginia Darden School of Business (Coursera)

☐ Negotiation
Successful Negotiation: Essential Skills and Strategies • Professor George Siedel, University of Michigan (Coursera)

☐ Business ethics
New Models of Business in Society • Professor R. Freeman, University of Virginia Darden School of Business (Coursera)

CONCENTRATION COURSES

☐ Branding
Digital Branding and Engagement • Professor Sonia Dickinson, Curtin University (edX)

☐ Marketing
Digital Marketing Specialization (6 courses) • University of Illinois (Coursera)

Sample Course List 4, Concentration: Management and Leadership

FOUNDATION COURSES

❑ **Self-directed learning**
Learning How to Learn: Powerful Mental Tools to Help You Master Tough Subjects • Professors Barbara Oakley and Terry Sejnowski, University of California San Diego (Coursera)

❑ **Operations management**
Introduction to Operations Management • Professor Christian Terwiesch, University of Pennsylvania Wharton School of Business (Coursera)

❑ **Project management**
Fundamentals of Project Planning and Management • Professor Yael Grushka-Cockayne, University of Virginia Darden School of Business (Coursera)

❑ **Business strategy**
Foundations of Business Strategy • Professor Michael Lenox, University of Virginia Darden School of Business (Coursera)

❑ **Communication**
Leadership Communication for Maximum Impact: Storytelling • Professor Tom Collinger, Northwestern University (Coursera)

SKILL-BUILDING AND ELECTIVE COURSES

❑ **Human resources management**
Managing Talent • Professors Scott DeRue, Maxim Sytch, and Cheri Alexander, University of Michigan Ross School of Business (Coursera)

❑ **Management theory**
Critical Perspectives on Management • Professor Rolf Strom-Olsen, IE Business School (Coursera)

❑ **Negotiation**
Successful Negotiation: Essential Skills and Strategies • Professor George Siedel, University of Michigan (Coursera)

❏ **Business ethics**
The Three-Pillar Model for Business Decisions: Strategy, Law, and Ethics • Professor George Siedel, University of Michigan (Coursera)

❏ **Design thinking**
Design Kit: The Course for Human-Centered Design • IDEO.org, +Acumen (NovoEd)

CONCENTRATION COURSES

❏ **Strategy**
Competitive Strategy and Organization Design Specialization (4 courses) • Ludwig-Maximilians-Universität München (Coursera)

❏ **Leadership and management**
Strategic Leadership and Management Specialization (7 courses) • University of Illinois (Coursera)

APPENDIX D

For Further Reading

Bock, Laszlo. *Work Rules! Insights from Inside Google That Will Transform How You Live and Lead.* New York: Grand Central Publishing, 2015.

Clark, Dorie. *Reinventing You: Define Your Brand, Imagine Your Future.* Boston: Harvard Business Review Press, 2013.

Craig, Ryan. *College Disrupted: The Great Unbundling of Higher Education.* New York: Macmillan, 2015.

Grant, Adam. *Give and Take: Why Helping Others Drives Our Success.* New York: Viking/Penguin, 2013.

Kaufman, Josh. *The Personal MBA: Master the Art of Business.* New York: Portfolio/Penguin, 2012.

Mintzberg, Henry. *Managers Not MBAs: A Hard Look at the Soft Practice of Managing and Management Development.* San Francisco: Berrett-Koehler Publishers, 2005.

Oakley, Barbara. *Mindshift: Break Through Obstacles to Learning and Discover Your Hidden Potential.* New York: TarcherPerigee/Penguin, 2017.

Pink, Daniel. *To Sell Is Human: The Surprising Truth About Persuading, Convincing, and Influencing Others.* New York: Riverhead Books/Penguin, 2012.

Rath, Tom. *StrengthsFinder 2.0.* New York: Gallup Press, 2013.

Reis, Eric. *The Lean Startup: How Today's Entrepreneurs Use Continuous Innovation to Create Radically Successful Businesses.* New York: Crown Business, 2011.

Shell, G. Richard. *Springboard: Launching Your Personal Search for Success.* New York: Portfolio/Penguin, 2013.

APPENDIX E

Resources at NoPayMBA.com

You will find these additional resources to support your studies on my website, NoPayMBA.com.

Portfolio

No-Pay MBA offers a portfolio feature, where you can upload course certificates, projects, and examples of your work and arrange your portfolio according to the key skill sets you have developed during your studies. Register for your free portfolio at NoPayMBA.com/portfolio.

Facebook Group

The No-Pay MBA Facebook group provides a forum where you can meet other independent business students, ask questions, form a learning group, and share stories and articles. Join by clicking at NoPayMBA.com/book or at Facebook.com/groups/NoPayMBA.

Visit www.NoPayMBA.com/book to find out more.

NOTES AND REFERENCES

INTRODUCTION

1. Bureau of Labor Statistics, "News Release: Number of Jobs Held, Labor Market Activity, and Earnings Growth Among the Youngest Baby Boomers: Results from a Longitudinal Study," March 31, 2015, http://www.bls.gov/news.release/pdf/nlsoy.pdf.
2. Laszlo Bock, *Work Rules!: Insights from Inside Google That Will Transform How You Live and Lead* (New York: Grand Central Publishing, 2015), 66.
3. Ed Batista, "Should You Get an MBA?" *Harvard Business Review*, September 4, 2014, https://hbr.org/2014/09/should-you-get-an-mba.
4. "Business School Career and Salary, San Diego State University," *U.S. News and World Report*, accessed January 4, 2017, http://premium.usnews.com/best-graduate-schools/top-business-schools/san-diego-state-university-01024/salary-stats. Note: Premium, subscription only link.
5. Laurent Ortmans, "MBA by the Numbers: Inside the $200,000 Cost," *Financial Times*, February 14, 2016, https://www.ft.com/content/f6696828-be05-11e5-846f-79b0e3d20eaf#axzz40Hgqxg9w.
6. Anant Agarwal, "Unbundled: Reimagining Higher Education," *Huffington Post*, December 9, 2013, http://www.huffingtonpost.com/anant-agarwal/unbundled-reimagining-higher-education_b_4414048.html.

CHAPTER 1

1. Carol Dweck, *Mindset: The New Psychology of Success* (New York: Ballantine Books, 2006).
2. Steve Jobs, interview by David Sheff, *Playboy Magazine*, February 1985.

CHAPTER 2

1. Laura Pappano, "The Year of the MOOC," *New York Times*, November 2, 2012, http://www.nytimes.com/2012/11/04/education/edlife/massive-open-online-courses-are-multiplying-at-a-rapid-pace.html?_r=0.
2. Chris Parr, "Mooc Creators Criticise Courses' Lack of Creativity," *Times Higher Education*, October 17, 2013, https://www.times highereducation.com/news/mooc-creators-criticise-courses-lack-of-creativity/2008180.article.
3. John Markoff, "Visual and Artificial, but 58,000 Want Course," *New York Times*, August 15, 2011, http://www.nytimes.com/2011/08/16/science/16stanford.html.
4. Andrew Ng and Jennifer Widom, "Origins of the Modern MOOC (xMOOC)," accessed August 10, 2016, http://www. andrewng.org/?portfolio=origins-of-the-modern-mooc-xmooc.
5. Dhawal Shah, "By the Numbers: MOOCs in 2015," December 21, 2015, https://www.class-central.com/report/moocs-2015-stats/.

CHAPTER 3

1. J. Duncan Herrington, "MBA: Past Present and Future," *Academy of Educational Leadership Journal* 14, no. 1 (2010): 63–76.
2. Yale School of Management, "MBA," accessed August 22, 2016, http://som.yale.edu/programs/mba.
3. MIT Sloan School of Management, "MBA Program," accessed August 22, 2016, http://mitsloan.mit.edu/mba/.

CHAPTER 4

1. Ryan Craig, *College Disrupted: The Great Unbundling of Higher Education* (New York: St. Martin's Press, 2015), chap. 11, 3rd section.
2. Ryan Craig and Daniel Pianko, "Death of the Degree? Not So Fast," *Inside Higher Ed,* November 16, 2012, https://www.insidehighered.com/views/2012/11/16/disruption-will-make-degrees-more-valuable-not-less-essay.
3. Michelle Weise, "The Real Revolution in Online Education Isn't MOOCs," *Harvard Business Review*, October 17, 2014, https://hbr.org/2014/10/the-real-revolution-in-online-education-isnt-moocs.
4. Craig Hickman, *Mind of a Manager, Soul of a Leader* (New York: Wiley, 1992).
5. Douglas Martin, "Ed Sabol, Who Elevated Football Founding NFL Films, Dies at 98," *New York Times*, February 9, 2015, http://www.nytimes.com/2015/02/10/sports/football/ed-sabol-nfl-films-founder-dies-at-98.html?_r=0.

CHAPTER 5

1. Eric Reis, *The Lean Startup: How Today's Entrepreneurs Use Continuous Innovation to Create Radically Successful Businesses* (New York: Crown Business, 2011).
2. Jeanne Liedtka, *Design Thinking for Innovation*, Coursera, accessed January 5, 2017, https://www.coursera.org/learn/uva-darden-design-thinking-innovation.
3. Steve Jobs, "'You've Got to Find What You Love,' Jobs Says," *Stanford News*, June 14, 2005, http://news.stanford.edu/2005/06/14/jobs-061505/.
4. NYU Robert F. Wagner Graduate School of Public Service, "Tracks Exercise," 2013, http://wagner.nyu.edu/files/careers/TracksExercise.pdf.
5. Richard Dobbs, Jaana Remes, and Jonathan Woetzel, "Where to Look for Global Growth," *McKinsey Quarterly*, January 2015, http://www.mckinsey.com/global-themes/employment-and-growth/where-to-look-for-global-growth.
6. Andy Kiersz, "The 21 Best Jobs of the Future," *Business Insider*, December 14, 2015, http://www.businessinsider.com/the-21-best-jobs-of-the-future-2015-12/.

CHAPTER 6

1. Robert Putnam, *Bowling Alone: The Collapse and Revival of American Community* (New York: Simon and Schuster, 2000).
2. Susan Adams, "New Survey: LinkedIn More Dominant Than Ever Among Job Seekers and Recruiters, but Facebook Poised to Gain," *Forbes*, February 5, 2013, http://www.forbes.com/sites/susanadams/2013/02/05/new-survey-linked-in-more-dominant-than-ever-among-job-seekers-and-recruiters-but-facebook-poised-to-gain/.
3. Andrew Jefferson Hill, "Social Learning in Massive Open Online Courses: An Analysis of Pedagogical Implications and Students' Learning Experiences," in *UCLA Electronic Theses and Dissertations* (Los Angeles: UC Los Angeles, 2015), http://escholarship.org/uc/item/6qr7p6rq.
4. Mimi Zheng, "How 1 Tweet Led to an Internship in Silicon Valley," *Huffington Post*, October 23, 2016, http://www.huffingtonpost.com/mimi-zheng/how-1-tweet-led-to-an-int_b_12584624.html.

CHAPTER 7

1. Portfolium, "About Us," accessed January 6, 2017, https://portfolium.com/about.

CHAPTER 8

1. Christian Terwiesch, "Wharton Business Professor on MOOCs and the Future of the MBA," *No-Pay MBA* (blog),.February 24, 2015,

https://www.nopaymba.com/wharton-business-professor-moocs-future-mba/.

2. Michael Spence, "Job Market Signaling," *Quarterly Journal of Economics* 87, no. 3 (August, 1973): 355–374.

3. "Keeping an Eye on Recruiter Behavior: New Study Clarifies Recruiter Decision-Making," *TheLadders.com*, March 2012, https://cdn.theladders.net/static/images/basicSite/pdfs/TheLadders-EyeTracking-StudyC2.pdf.

CHAPTER 9

1. Quentin Hardy, "Gearing Up for the Cloud, AT&T Tells Its Workers: Adapt or Else," *New York Times*, February 13, 2016, http://www.nytimes.com/2016/02/14/technology/gearing-up-for-the-cloud-att-tells-its-workers-adapt-or-else.

2. Jen Hubley Luckwaldt, "5 High-Paying Jobs That Didn't Exist 10 Years Ago," *Payscale.com*, 2015, http://www.payscale.com/career-news/2015/09/5-high-paying-jobs-that-didnt-exist-10-years-ago.

3. Peter High, "MIT Team Turns 6.9 Million Clicks into Insights to Improve Online Education," *Forbes*, August 11, 2014, http://www.forbes.com/sites/peterhigh/2014/08/11/mit-team-turns-6-9-million-clicks-into-insights-to-improve-online-education/#69119421b0eb.

4. Degreed.com, "Manifesto," accessed December 14, 2016, https://degreed.com/about.

5. Dhawal Shah, "Monetization over Massiveness: A Review of MOOC Stats and Trends in 2016," *Class Central*, accessed January 2, 2017, https://www.class-central.com/report/moocs-stats-and-trends-2016/.

CONCLUSION

1. Katty Kay and Claire Shipman, "The Confidence Gap," *The Atlantic*, May 2014.

INDEX